*Black Immigration
and Ethnicity
in the
United States*

**Bibliographies and Indexes in Afro-American and African Studies**

Black-Jewish Relations in the United States: A Selected Bibliography
*Compiled by Lenwood G. Davis*

# Black Immigration and Ethnicity in the United States

*An Annotated Bibliography*

Center for Afroamerican
and African Studies,
The University of Michigan

Bibliographies and Indexes in Afro-American and African Studies, Number 2

*Greenwood Press*
Westport, Connecticut • London, England

**Library of Congress Cataloging in Publication Data**

Main entry under title:

Black immigration and ethnicity in the United States.

(Bibliographies and indexes in Afro-American and
African studies, ISSN 0742-6925 ; no. 2)
  1. Blacks—United States—Bibliography.  2. Afro-
Americans—Bibliography.   3. United States—Foreign
population—Bibliography.   4. United States—Emigration
and immigration—Bibliography.  I. University of Michigan.
Center for Afroamerican and African Studies.  II. Series.
Z1361.N39B553 1984    [E185]    016.3058'96073    84-12886
ISBN  0-313-24366-2  (lib. bdg.)

Library of Congress Catalog Card Number: 84-12886
ISBN:   0-313-24366-2
ISSN:   0742-6925

First published in 1985

Greenwood Press
A division of Congressional Information Service, Inc.
88 Post Road West, Westport, Connecticut 06881

Printed in the United States of America

10  9  8  7  6  5  4  3  2  1

# Contents

# Acknowledgments

Tao Lin Huang, Center Research Assistant and graduate student in the Department of Anthropology, has been primarily responsible for compiling and annotating the references in this Bibliography. Graduate Assistant Debbie Robinson prepared the indexes and supervised the final manuscript preparation. Research Assistants Malaika Wangara and Bradford Pollack also participated at various times in the literature surveys. Overall supervision for this project has been the responsibility of Shirley A. Clarkson. Everyone involved in the project owes a debt of gratitude to Linda Largin, the word processor, who prepared the copy.

Finally, the Center gratefully acknowledges the support of The University of Michigan's College of Literature, Science, and Arts and Horace H. Rackham School of Graduate Studies, which made preparation of the Bibliography possible.

# Introduction

This volume attempts to present a comprehensive bibliography of literature, both scholarly and journalistic, related to the issues of Black immigration of recent decades and its effects on the changing composition of the Black population in the United States. It is compiled by the Center for Afroamerican and African Studies of the University of Michigan as a service to the scholarly community and the general public interested in academic research and policy discussion on this subject. This Bibliography, therefore, aims to provide an overview of the subject matter, review the achievements of research so far, identify significant gaps in the literature, and enlighten discussion and deliberation on related policy issues.

Although the immigration of peoples of African descent to the United States is a historically continuous phenomenon, the number of immigrants has significantly increased and their countries of origin diversified since the end of World War II. This is even more pronounced following the change of U.S. immigration policy in 1965. Since then, there have been ever growing streams of immigrants from the Caribbean and from the African continent itself. Although not all of these immigrants are regarded, or regard themselves, as "Blacks," a significant proportion of them share varying degrees of African ancestry and have come from areas with significant proportions of Blacks in their populations. All of them have come to this country with distinctive historical and cultural backgrounds, with different conceptions of racial and ethnic identity, and with varying aspirations for adapting to the host society.

The backgrounds of these immigrants, their lives in the United States, and the changes they have wrought in American society as a whole are clear issues of considerable importance for both scholarly research and policymaking. Even more significant is the need to systematically study these new immigrants in their relationships to the indigenous Black population, which can no longer be conceived of as an ethnically and culturally homogenous group. Diversity, as much as unity, within this group is an urgent topic for careful research and assessment. Questions regarding the historical and contemporary bases of Black ethnic diversity, its magnitude, its implications for comparative discussions of ethnicity and ethnic relations in America and elsewhere, and its relevance for the formulation and implementation of public policies and programs are central issues that need to be explored in future research.

We offer this Bibliography therefore, as a survey of literature as well as a catalyst for further research. The works listed and annotated in this volume deal with topics ranging from the general theoretical subjects of immigration, ethnicity, and identity, U.S. immigration policies, the various aspects of immigrant experience, to specific immigrant groups in the United States through 1982.

In selecting titles for inclusion in this Bibliography, we have made a survey of library catalogs as well as the various abstracts in the social sciences and history. Major scholarly journals and selected popular magazines have also been searched systematically. We have consulted the computerized data base of the Library of Congress for periodic literature and government documents. Pertinent dissertations are selected from the listings in Dissertation Abstract International, each dissertation is provided with a number (preceded by the letters DAI) indicating the page of DAI on which the abstract is located. To assist the user, we have included the Superintendent of Documents Number (SuDoc Number) when available, for government document citations.

Of the 1,049 citations, approximately half are annotated. Selection for annotation is based on the title's significance in itself as well as it's usefulness for comparative purposes. No critical evaluation is attempted in the annotations. In most cases, the annotations are written after reading the works in question. In cases where they were not directly available we have relied on abstracts and reference sources for the annotations.

In its overall organization this Bibliography is divided into six sections, moving from more general to more specific subject matters.

Part I lists bibliographies and literature surveys relevant to the study of Black immigration and ethnicity. Part II includes citations of general works on immigration and ethnicity selected from significant contributions published in the past two decades.

Part III includes citations on U.S. immigration legislation and policies. It contains not only selected official documents such as congressional hearings and governmental publications but also critical analyses and commentaries. Selection is especially focused on works dealing with post-1965 policy developments related to immigration from the Caribbean and Africa.

Part IV consists of references pertinent to the study of Black and other recent immigrants to the United States. It is organized according to specific areas of analysis as follows: history; demography and settlement patterns; employment and economics; education, health, and social services; language and bilingualism; political behavior and organization; and literature of immigrant experience. There are a number of works that could have been listed in this section, but because they deal with specific Black immigrant groups we have chosen to list them in Part V, "Studies of Black Immigrant Groups."

Part V, the largest and core section of the present volume, is devoted to works on the various immigrant groups in the United States that include significant numbers of Blacks. An attempt has been made to include all works dealing specifically with Black immigrants as well as key references on immigrant groups as a whole from the Caribbean and Africa. It should be pointed out that, as the racial and ethnic identities of portions of these groups are a matter at issue, we have included some studies whose relevance to Black immigration and ethnicity may not be apparent.

The sixth and final section lists, for comparative purposes, selected references on Black immigration to other countries, Canada and Great Britain in particular.

Works are cited only once, although, as can be expected, some may fit in more than one category.  Therefore, author and subject indexes are provided that refer to appropriate entry numbers in the Bibliography.

Niara Sudarkasa, Director
Center for Afroamerican and African Studies

October 1983

# I.
# Bibliographies and Surveys of Literature

0001. "Annotated Bibliography on Puerto Rico and Puerto Rican Migration."
International Migration Review, Vol. 2, No. 2 (Spring 1968), pp. 96-102.

This bibliography was intended to serve as a complement and a guide to the
studies on Puerto Rican migration published in the Spring, 1968 issue of The
International Migration Review. The titles are of general interest in the
areas of the cultural, social, economic, and political life on the Island and on
the mainland.

0002. Bentley, G. Carter. Ethnicity and Nationality: A Bibliographic Guide.
Seattle: University of Washington Press, 1982. 456 pp.

This bibliography seeks to organize and structure the literature on ethnicity
and nationality which has been, for the most part, characterized as internally
unorganized and diffuse. To accomplish this goal, detailed area and content
indexes are utilized. The area index classifies sources by continent, region,
country, and where warranted, by individual ethnic group. The content index
classifies citations according to sources of data, the scale of analysis, academic
field, theoretical orientation, as well as the more traditional sociological,
political, and cultural themes. These indexes not only appear in the appendix,
but each citation is coded with this information. Of the 2,338 citations
included, 308 contain comprehensive annotations.

0003. Berry-Caban, C.S. Hispanics in Wisconsin: A Bibliography of Resource
Materials. Madison: The State Historical Society of Wisconsin, 1981. 258 pp.

Includes citations of virtually all materials pertaining to Wisconsin's hispanic
population (Mexican, Puerto Rican and Cuban) which have appeared in newspapers, journals, manuscripts, collections, theses, reports and photographs.
Introduction and subject headings in English and Spanish.

0004. Brana-Shute, Rosemary. A Bibliography of Caribbean Migration and Caribbean
Immigrant Communities. Bibliographic Series Number 9. Gainsville, FL: University
of Florida Libraries and University at Florida Center for Latin American Studies,
1983. 339 pp.

This bibliography includes works on the migration of people into, within, and
out of the Caribbean region. In efforts to represent the heterogenity which
has resulted from this type of migration, literature in many languages is

referenced (English, French, Spanish, Dutch, German, Italian, Slovak, Polish and Welsh).  Unique indices of origin of migrant and destination of migrant are also included.

0005.  Buenker, J. D. and Burckel, N. C.  Immigration and Ethnicity: A Guide to Information Sources.  Detroit: Gale Research Co., 1977. 305 pp.

0006.  Caroli, Betty Boyd.  "Recent Immigration to the United States."  Trends in History: A Review of Current Periodical Literature in History, Vol. 2, No. 4 (Summer 1982), pp. 49-69.

Bibliographic essay which covers works pertaining to the 1965 Immigration Law, its effect on specific immigrant groups, "The Brain Drain", and illegal immigration.  Twenty-three journals were consulted for this review.

0007.  Casal, Lourdes and Hernandes, Andres R.  "Cubans in the U.S.: A Survey of Literature."  Cuban Studies/Estudios Cubanos, Vol. 5, No. 2 (July 1975), pp. 25-51.

0008.  Cordasco, Francesco.  Immigrant Children in American Schools.  A Classified and Annotated Bibliography with Selected Source Documents.  Fairfield, NJ: Augustus M. Kelley, Publishers, 1976.  381 pp.

0009.  Cordasco, Francesco.  "Bilingual Education in American Schools: A Bibliographical Essay."  The Immigration History Newsletter, Vol. 14, No. 1 (May 1982), pp. 1-8.

This bibliographic essay discusses American bilingual programs, ESL theory and evaluation instruments, the controversey surrounding bilingual education, bilingual programs for those other than spanish-speaking, legislation related to bilingual programs, and suggests guides to information about ethnic groups in general.

0010.  Cordasco, Francesco and Bernstein, George.  Bilingual Education in American Schools: A Guide to Information Sources.  Detroit:  Gale Research Co., 1979. 307 pp.

0011.  Cordasco, F.; Bucchioni, E. and Castellanos, D.  Puerto Ricans on the U.S. Mainland:  A Bibliography of Reports, Texts, Critical Studies, and Related Materials.  Totowa, NJ:  Rowman and Littlefield, 1972. 146 pp.

This work selectively highlights literature dealing with Puerto Ricans on the island, their migration to the U.S., and their mainland experience (acculturation, education, health and employment).  Included are 754 English and Spanish citations.  Many of which are annotated.

0012.  "Cubans in the U.S.: A Selected Bibliography."  NCCA News (National Center for Community Action News), No. 3-4 (September-October 1978), pp. 4-6.

0013.  Davidson, C. and Charles, H.  "Caribbean Migration to the U.S.: A Selected Bibliography."  In Caribbean Migration to the United States.  Eds., R.S. Bryce-Laporte and D.M. Mortimer. Washington, DC:  Smithsonian Institution, Research Institute on Immigration and Ethnic Stuides,  Occasional Papers No.  1, 1976.

This annotated bibliography is one of the first to compile and review the literature on the new wave of Caribbean migration to the United States.

The detailed annotations include, for the most part, the original abstract from the researcher. They outline the authors purpose, findings, and conclusions.

0014. Fox, James W. Illegal Immigration: A Bibliography, 1968-1978. Monticello, IL: Vance Bibliographies, 1978. 32 pp.

0015. Goldberg, Gertrude S. "Puerto Rican Migrants on the Mainland of the United States: A Review of the Literature." IRCD Bulletin (Information Retrival Center on the Disadvantaged, Yeshiva University, New York), Vol. 4, No. 1 (January 1968), pp. 1-12.

0016. Hellwig, David J. "Afro-American Views of Immigrants, 1830-1930: A Historiographical-Bibliographical Essay." The Immigration History Newsletter, Vol. 13, No. 2 (November 1981), pp. 1-5.

Critical bibliographic essay which reviews the literature on immigrants' reaction to Black Americans, noting paucity of literature on the reaction of Blacks to newcomers. Although the author discusses Blacks' reaction to Irish, Italians, Jews, and Chinese, his review of works on Blacks views of West Indians is most pertinent.

0017. Herrera, D., ed. Puerto Ricans and Other Minority Groups in the Continental United States: An Annotated Bibliography. Detroit: Blaine Ethridge Books, 1979. 397 pp.

Although majority of the 2,155 works cited relate to the educational experience of Puerto Rican children in the United States (with special emphasis on educational testing, bilingual education, cognitive style, and teacher training) many citations have historical, economic, sociological, and anthropological relevance to the Puerto Rican experience as a whole. Most of the citations are annotated.

0018. Johnson, Harry A. Ethnic American Minorities: A Guide to Media and Materials. New York: R.R. Bowker, 1976. 304 pp.

The ethnic groups covered in this work include Afro-Americans, Asian Americans, Native Indians, and Spanish Speaking Americans (Mexicans, Cuban and Puerto Ricans). There is a descriptive section for each group which gives a brief history, a current demographic profile, and includes a discussion of particular characteristics and needs of the group. The genere of media cited include films, filmstrips, slides, transparencies, records, audio and video cassettes as well as posters and graphics. In addition the year and rental/purchase information, the annotations give the grade level for which material is appropriate.

0019. Kinton, J. F. American Ethnic Groups, A Sourcebook for the 1970's. Mt. Pleasant, IA: Social Science and Sociological Resources, 1973. 148 pp.

Includes citations not only on 24 ethnic groups (including Puerto Rican), but also on ethnic group theory, and race relations. The sourcebook includes all sociological works and major pieces from anthropology and American history that focus on ethnic and racial studies; theoretical and empirical.

0020. Kolm, Richard. Bibliography on Ethnicity and Ethnic Groups. Washington, DC: U.S. Government Printing Office, 1973. 250 pp. (SuDoc Number: HE 20.2417: Et3)

Primary emphasis given to two major subject areas: materials dealing with the situation of immigrant ethnic groups, their psychological adjustment and conditions affecting acculturation; and materials dealing with patterns of ethnic behavior, identity, family life, and communication structure. One fourth of the 1,694 citations are annotated.

0021. Meadows, Paul et al., eds. Recent Immigration to the United States: The Literature of the Social Sciences. Washington, DC: Smithsonian Institution, Research Institute on Immigration and Ethnic Studies, Bibliographic Studies No. 1, 1976.

0022. Miller, Wayne C. et al. A Comprehensive Bibliography for the Study of American Minorities. New York: New York University Press, 1976. 2 vols., 1380 pp.

0023. Mortimer, Delores M. "Women and Migration : A Bibliography." In Female Immigrants to the United States: Caribbean, Latin American, and African Experiences. Eds. D. M. Mortimer and R. S. Bryce-Laporte. Washington, DC: Smithsonian Institution, Research Institute on Immigration and Ethnic Studies, Occasional Papers No. 2, 1981, pp. 364-482.

First and only major bibliographic work which focuses on issues of gender, race and immigration. Includes 630 references of which one-third are annotated.

0024. North, Jeannette H. Immigration Literature: Abstracts of Demographic, Economic, and Policy Studies. Washington, DC: Government Printing Office, 1979. 89 pp. (SuDoc Number: J21.16: Im6)

0025. Oaks, Priscilla. Minority Studies: A Selective Annotated Bibliography. Boston: G.K. Hall, 1975. 303 pp.

0026. The Puerto Ricans: Migration and General Bibliography. New York: Arno Press, 1975. 55 pp.

0027. Schander, Edwin R. "Immigration Law and Practice in the United States: A Selective Bibliography." International Migration Review, Vol. 12, No. 1 (Spring 1978), pp. 117-127.

This selective bibliography attempts to bring together relevant material, monographs and periodicals from the realm of law literature on immigration that may be of interest to members of the legal profession as well as to scholars in law related fields of migration studies. The scope of this bibliography is limited to the review of the currently available legal literature of the period 1970 through December 1977.

0028. Senior, C. Annotated Bibliography on Puerto Ricans in the United States. Puerto Rico: Department of Migration, Migration Division. 1959. 37 pp.

0029. Stobin, Leslie Gail. International Alien Labor Problems and Solutions: A Bibliography, 1960-1980. Monticello, IL: Vance Bibliographies, 1980. 15 pp.

0030. Vivo, Paquita, ed. The Puerto Ricans: An Annotated Bibliography. New York: R.R. Bowker, 1973. 267 pp.

This bibliography demonstrates bredth through the subjects covered, the time period examined (pre-Colombian era through contemporary political thought and economic development), and in the type of work included (books, dissertations, government publication - U.S. and Puerto Rican, journals, magazines, as well as filmstrips and movies).  It includes both English and Spanish citations.  The work is completely annotated except for a subset of citations within the literature section.

# II.
# General Literature on Immigration and Ethnicity

# 1.
# Immigration and Immigrant Populations

0031. Avila, Fernando Bastos de. Economic Impacts of Immigration. Westport, CT: Greenwood Press, 1970. 102 pp.

0032. Bach, Robert L. and Schraml, Lisa A. "Migration, Crisis, and Theoretical Conflict." International Migration Review, Vol. 16, No. 2 (Summer 1982), pp. 320-341.

This article examines the theoretical and political differences between the equilibrium and historical-structuralist perspectives on international migration. The authors also criticize the shortcomings of a third position which proposes to use the household as the basic unit of analysis, pointing out its too narrow emphasis on individual decision-making and calculations.

0033. Bentz, Thomas. New Immigrants: Portraits in Passage. New York: The Pilgrim Press, 1981. 209 pp.

Thirteen immigrant families talk about their reasons for emigrating and their adaptation in the United States. In each chapter the members of one family discuss with the author their problems and hopes. Immigrants from China, Korea, Vietnam, Laos, the Philippines, Samoa, Cuba, Haiti, Mexico, and Chile are interviewed.

0034. Bouvier, L. F. et al. "International Migration: Yesterday, Today, and Tomorrow." Population Bulletin, Vol. 32 (1977), pp. 2-42.

0035. Breton, Raymond. "Institutional Completeness of Ethnic Communities and the Personal Relations of Immigrants." American Journal of Sociology, Vol. 70, No. 2 (September 1964), pp. 193-205.

This study, based on interview data from Montreal, analyzes the focus of immigrant interpersonal relations—they can be integrated within the native community, within their ethnic community, or within a group of immigrants of a different ethnicity. The focus of integration is only partially determined by the characteristics of the immigrant. The principal determinant is the ability of the ethnic community to attract immigrants which depends on its degree of institutional completeness.

0036. Brody, E. B. Behavior in New Environments: Adaptation of Migrant Populations. Beverly Hills: Sage Publications, 1970. 479 pp.

0037. Bryce-Laporte, Roy S. "Visibility of the New Immigrants." Transaction/-Society, Vol. 14, No. 6 (September/October 1977), pp. 18-22.

New immigrants entering the U.S. after the 1965 Immigration Act are notable for their increased visibility in comparison to earlier immigrants. These groups challenge the traditional U.S. views on race, ethnicity and culture requiring greater equality and change in that tradition. The new immigrants will contribute to increasing tensions between two American traditions: the myth of equal opportunity on the one hand, and the reality of inequality of opportunities on the other.

0038. Bryce-Laporte, Roy S. "On the Presence, Migrations, and Cultures of Blacks in the Americas: Some Imperatives for Afro-Hispanic American Studies." Caribe, Vol. 4 (1979), pp. 10-18.

0039. Bryce-Laporte, Roy S. "Introduction: The New Immigration: The Female Majority." In Female Immigrants to the United States. Eds., D. M. Mortimer and R. S. Bryce-Laporte. Washington, DC: Smithsonian Institution, Research Institute on Immigration and Ethnic Studies, Occasional Papers No. 2, 1981, pp. vii-xxxix.

Emphasizes that after 1965 the majority of immigrants to the U.S. have been women—the male-female ratio among the immigrants being roughly 2 to 3. Advocates scholarly study of the experience of these female and mostly black immigrants. The article also summarizes the papers collected in the volume.

0040. Bryce-Laporte, R. S., ed. Sourcebook on the New Immigration: Implications for the United States and the International Community. Washington, DC: Smithsonian Institution, Research Institute on Immigration and Ethnic Studies, 1979. 511 pp.

The Sourcebook is a collection of papers from the Research Institute on Immigration and Ethnic Studies (RIIES) seminal conference on post 1965 immigration to the United States. Valuable bibliographic notes are included.

0041. Bryce-Laporte, R. S., ed. Sourcebook on the New Immigration: Supplement. Washington, DC: Smithsonian Institution, Research Institute on Immigration and Ethnic Studies, 1979. 302 pp.

0042. Carruthers, Norman and Vining, Aidan R. "International Migration: An Application of the Urban Location Choice Model." World Politics, Vol. 35, No. 1 (October 1982), pp. 106-120.

This paper argues that the urban location choice model provides a theory that integrates economic and political models of migration, and more appropriately measures all economic costs and benefits.

0043. Castles, Stephen and Kosack, Godula. Immigrant Workers and Class Structure in Western Europe. London: Oxford University Press, 1973. 514 pp.

0044. Chaney, Elsa M. "The World Economy and Contemporary Migration. Foreword." International Migration Review, Vol. 13, No. 2 (Summer 1979), pp. 204-212.

The author argues that recent migrations of Caribbean and Latin American peoples to the United States are the direct result of the disparity in growth between developed and developing countries. She argues that such large-scale movements of people constitute international proletarian diasporas which call for establishing greater equality between and within societies, under conditions of a cultural pluralism.

0045. Chaney, Elsa M. Women in International Migration: Issues in Development Planning. Washington, DC: Office of Women in Development, U.S. Agency for International Development, 1980.

0046. Commons, J. R. Races and Immigrants in America. Fairfield, NJ: Augustus M. Kelley, 1967. 242 pp.

0047. Contemporary Marxism "The New Nomads: Immigration and Changes in the International Division of Labor." No. 5 (Summer 1982), pp. 1-119.

0048. Cornelius, Wayne A. "Interviewing Undocumented Immigrants: Methodological Reflections Based on Fieldwork in Mexico and the U.S." International Migration Review, Vol. 16, No. 2 (Summer 1982), pp. 378-411.

Reviews data collection methods and discusses basic issues of research strategy in field studies of undocumented immigrants. Suggests ways to increase the reliability and validity of interview responses.

0049. Couch, Stephen R. and Bryce-Laporte, Roy S., eds. Quantitative Data and Immigration Research. Washington, DC: Smithsonian Institution, Research Institute on Immigration and Ethnic Studies, Research Notes No. 2, 1979. 294 pp.

Articles grouped into three sections dealing with: (1) availability and sources of quantitative data; (2) characteristics and limitations of available data; and (3) techniques for using such data in the study of Caribbean migration.

0050. Dinnerstein, L. and Jaher, F. C., eds. The Aliens: A History of Ethnic Minorities in America. New York: Appleton-Century-Crofts, 1970. 347 pp.

0051. Dinnerstein, L. and Reimers, D. M. Ethnic Americans: A History of Immigration and Assimilation. New York: Harper and Row, 1975. Second edition, 1981. 174 pp.

0052. Du Toit, B. M. and Safa, H. I., eds. Migration and Urbanization: Models and Adaptive Strategies. The Hauge: Mouton, 1976. 305 pp.

0053. Fitzpatrick, Joseph P. "The Importance of 'Community' in the Process of Immigrant Assimilation." International Migration Review, Vol. 1, No. 1 (Fall 1966), pp. 5-16.

This paper attempts to clarify the concept of community, especially the problems of its identification, its boundaries, and its links to larger societies. The usefulness of the concept for the study of cultural assimilation is emphasized, since the community provides for the immigrant a base of security, and psycho-social satisfaction while he/she learns to adjust to the new society.

0054. Glazer, William A. The Brain Drain: Emigration and Return. Oxford: Pergamon Press, 1978. 324 pp.

This study is based on data collected in a multi-national survey conducted in the 1970's. 6,550 respondents in Canada, France, and the U.S. from 11 developing nations, as well as professionals who had returned home to their countries, were surveyed. This study includes consideration of social factors and shows multiple motives for the respondents' decision to return home or stay abroad.

0055. Goldlust, J. and Richmond, A. H. "A Multivariate Model of Immigrant Adaptation." International Migration Review, Vol. 8, No. 2 (Summer 1974), pp. 193-225.

0056. Hellwig, David J. "The Afro-American and the Immigrant, 1880-1930: A Study of Black Social Thought." Ph.D. dissertation, Syracuse University, 1973. 298 pp. (DAI: 34/11A, p. 7151)

A historical analysis based on extensive use of Black newspapers and journals. Similarities and differences between Blacks and Whites in their reaction to immigration are examined. Compares Blacks' different reception of immigrants from Europe and from the West Indies.

0057. Hirschman, Charles. "Immigrants and Minorities: Old Questions for New Directions in Research." International Migration Review, Vol. 16, No. 2 (Summer 1982), pp. 474-490.

This article examines three sets of factors that are relevant to the study of immigrant and ethnic group socioeconomic progress: (1) the initial characteristics of the immigrants; (2) the structure of economic opportunities; and (3) the reception or response by the host or dominant population.

0058. Kessner, Thomas and Caroli, Betty Boyd. Today's Immigrants, Their Stories: A New Look at the Newest Americans. New York: Oxford University Press, 1981. 317 pp.

Life histories of some immigrants who came to the United States after 1965. The immigrant groups covered in this book include: Chinese, Korean, Indochinese, Russian Jew, Italian, Irish, Greek, Honduran, West Indian, and Peruvian. The authors' commentaries are intermixed with the immigrants' own accounts.

0059. Kramer, Judith. The American Minority Community. New York: Appleton-Century-Crofts, 1970. 293 pp.

0060. Kunz, E. F. "The Refugee in Flight: Kinetic Models and Forms of Displacement." International Migration Review, Vol. 7, No. 2 (Summer 1973). pp. 125-146.

0061. Lieberson, Stanley. A Piece of the Pie: Black and White Immigrants Since 1880. Berkeley: University of California Press, 1981. 419 pp.

This book deals with the questions about why "new" European immigrants fared so much better in the U.S. through the years than did Black migrants in the North. Drawing most of his data from U.S. censuses, Lieberson compares the two groups with regard to educational attainment, residential segregation, and occupational mobility. His evidence shows a deterioration in the position of Blacks over time in the North, particularly in the period after the 1930s. Racial discrimination and the timing of migration are emphasized as the major factors accounting for Black position.

0062. Massey, Douglas S. "Dimensions of the New Immigration to the United States and the Prospects for Assimilation." Annual Review of Sociology, Vol. 7 (1981), pp. 57-85.

This review draws upon research from a variety of disciplines and attempts to discover who the "new immigrants" are and how they are faring in the U.S. Compared to earlier immigrants, today's migrants comprise a broader mix of socioeconomic backgrounds, drawing on both ends of the educational and occupational spectrums, and are dispersed more widely throughout the country. On the whole, these new immigrant groups have shown trends toward assimilation to the host society. This assessment follows a discussion on six facets of assimilation: familism, fertility, residential segregation, political participation, intermarriage, and social mobility.

0063. Mortimer, Delores M. "Race, Ethnicity, and Sex in the Recent Immigration." In Female Immigrants to the United States: Caribbean, Latin American, and African Experiences. Eds., D. M. Mortimer and R. S. Bryce-Laporte. Washington, DC: Smithsonian Institution, Research Institute on Immigration and Ethnic Studies, Occasional Papers No. 2, 1981. pp. xi-lxvii.

The first part of this article stresses the dynamics and nuances of the categories of race, color, and ethnicity, in the immigrants' self-identification and their identification by others. The second briefly discusses aspects of the migration process as it applies to women, especially their roles in family and in employment. The author concludes that immigrant women will play a crucial role in the dynamics of ethnicity as well as in the struggle toward equalization between the sexes.

0064. Mortimer, Delores M. and Bryce-Laporte, Roy S., eds. Female Immigrants to the United States: Caribbean, Latin American, and African Experiences. Washington, D.C.: Smithsonian Institution, Research Institute on Immigration and Ethnic Studies, Occasional Papers No. 2, 1981. 487 pp.

0065. Piore, Michael P. Birds of Passage: Migrant Labor and Industrial Societies. Cambridge: Cambridge University Press, 1979. 229 pp.

An analytic framework is developed to explain the demand for migrant labor and the process of immigrant settlement. The demand for migrant labor derives from: (1) labor shortage; (2) the need to fill the bottom positions in the job hierarchy; and (3) the requirements of the secondary sector of a dual labor market. The immigrant settlement process is divided into an earlier, more transient phase and a later, more permanent one. Piore argues that permanent settlement is often not the initial intention of the immigrants, but rather an outcome forced upon them by circumstances. The characteristics of the immigrant's participation in the labor market is delineated in light of the above features. The impact of migration on doner countries is examined, and the history of U.S. immigration is used to illustrate the analytical framework. Finally, the author discusses some needed changes in U.S. immigration policy as called for by his theoretical arguments.

0066. Portes, Alejandro. "Migration and Underdevelopment." Politics and Society, Vol. 8, No. 1 (1978), pp. 1-48.

Migration plays two important roles in the development of the capitalist world system: it is a source of labor; and it is the way exploited classes in the periphery attempt to cope with the constraints of their situation. Such constraints are often manipulated to generate migration.

0067. Portes, Alejandro. "Toward a Structural Analysis of Illegal (Undocumented) Immigration." International Migration Review, Vol. 12, No. 4 (Winter 1978), pp. 469-485.

This paper discusses five basic propositions which will provide a framework for the analysis of illegal immigration. The two propositions concerning the receiving countries are: (1) the rate of return to capital is inversely related to the costs of labor; and (2) advanced capitalist societies tend to be characterized by scarcity of labor. There are three propositions concerning the sending countries: (1) international migration tends to originate in urbanizing and industrializing countries; (2) these countries tend to be characterized by an abundance of labor; and (3) industrialization in these countries is based on technologies associated with conditions of labor scarcity.

0068. Portes, Alejandro. "Illegal Immigration and the International System: Lessons from Recent Legal Mexican Immigrants to the United States." Social Problems, Vol. 26, No. 4 (April 1979), pp. 425-438.

Data from a 1972-73 sample of formerly undocumented Mexican immigrants indicate that a large segment has non-rural origins, comparatively high levels of education, industrial and service occupational backgrounds, and that most are headed for urban areas and occupations. These findings are contrary to conventional views about undocumented immigrants. They support the idea that immigration is an outgrowth of the accelerating contradictions brought about by capitalist development in Mexico and in other nations in the United States periphery.

0069. Portes, Alejandro. "Modes of Structural Incorporation and Present Theories of Labor Immigration." In Global Trends in Migration: Theory and Research of International Population Movements. New York: Center for Migration Studies, 1981, pp. 179-197.

0070. Portes, Alejandro; Parker, Robert N. and Cobas, Jose A. "Assimilation or Consciousness: Perceptions of U.S. Society Among Recent Latin American Immigrants to the United States." Social Forces, Vol. 59, No. 1 (1980), pp. 200-224.

Using interview data from samples of Mexican and Cuban immigrants, this paper examines two competing views of immigrant's perceptions of U.S. society and perception of discrimination: Assimilation theory vs. conflict theory. Findings lean in the direction of conflict theory which hypothesizes that greater familiarity with the culture and language and some economic advancement will lead to greater consciousness of the reality of discrimination and a more critical appraisal of the host society.

0071. Reid, Ira de Augustine. "Immigration and Assimilation." Current History, (Nov. 1955), pp. 305-310.

Historical experience has contradicted the expectancy that immigrants should be capable of "Anglo-conformity." Realities dictate that the uniformity of population and the total assimilation of immigrants as desirable national goals should be abandoned.

0072. Richmond, Anthony H. "Migration, Ethnicity and Race Relations." Ethnic and Racial Studies, Vol. 1, No. 1 (January 1978), pp. 1-18.

This paper presents a multivariate model of the immigrant adaptation process which incorporates both the situational factors in the host society and the pre-immigration characteristics of the immigrants themselves. This provides the framework for a general systems approach to the study of ethnic and race relations.

0073. Rosoff, Patricia; Zeisel, William and Quandt, Jean B., eds. Ethnic and Immigration Groups: Twentieth Century History and Comparative Analysis. New York: Hawarth Press, 1982.

0074. Safa, Helen I. and Du Toit, B. M., eds. Migration and Development: Implications for Ethnic Identity and Political Conflict. The Hague: Mouton, 1975. 336 pp.

0075. Sarna, Jonathan D. "From Immigrants to Ethnics: Toward a New Theory of 'Ethnicization'." Ethnicity, Vol. 5, No. 4 (December 1978), pp. 370-378.

The author contrasts the fragmented nature of immigrant groups upon their arrival in the U.S. with the social and cultural unities among ethnic groups years later. This process of "ethnicization" of immigrants is explained as a consequence of two factors: (1) the ascription of ethnic identity by the host society; (2) defense by immigrant institutions in the face of adversity.

0076. Senior, Clarence. "Migration as a Process and Migrant as a Person." Population Review, Vol. 6, No. 1 (1962), pp. 30-41.

A general discussion based on Puerto Rican migration to the U.S. and West Indian migration to the U.K.

0077. Smith, M. Estellie. "Networks and Migration Resettlement: Cherchez la Femme." Anthropological Quarterly, Vol. 49, No. 1 (January 1976), pp. 20-27.

0078. Taeuber, A. F. and Taeuber, K. E. "Recent Immigration and Studies of Ethnic Assimilation." Demography, Vol. 4, No. 2 (1967), pp. 298-308.

0079. Taeuber, Karl E. and Taeuber, Alma F. "The Negro as an Immigrant Group: Recent Trends in Racial and Ethnic Segregation in Chicago." American Journal of Sociology, Vol. 69, No. 4 (Jan. 1964), pp. 374-382.

Despite their social and economic progress, Black-American residential segregation remained very high. This persistence of residential segregation cannot be attributed to their low economic status alone. By contrast, residential desegregation and assimilation has continued to occur among immigrant groups, including Puerto Ricans and Mexicans.

0080. Tomasi, Silvano M. and Keely, Charles B. Whom Have We Welcomed? Staten Island, NY: Center for Migration Studies, 1975. 96 pp.

0081. Wood, Charles H. "Equilibrium and Historical-Structural Perspectives on Migration." International Migration Review, Vol. 16, No. 2 (Summer 1982), pp. 298-319.

The equilibrium model of labor mobility and the historical-structural perspective on population movement are critiqued. An alternative framework is presented which sees migration as an activity embedded in, and conditional upon, the success or failure of the initiatives undertaken by the household.

The author argues that the analysis of household sustenance strategies, interpreted within the context of the political economy, provides a more holistic approach than earlier perspectives.

# 2.
# Race, Ethnicity, and Identity

0082. Alcock, Anthony E. et al. The Future of Cultural Minorties. New York: St. Martin's Press, 1979. 221pp.

0083. Austin, B. William. "Why Ethnicity Is Important to Blacks." The Urban League Review, Vol. 1, No. 2 (Fall 1975), pp. 13-17.

> The author sees ethnic relationships as generalized kinship relations, and ethnic allegiance as an outgrowth of family solidarity. He maintains that not only do Blacks constitute an ethnic group vis-a-vis Whites, but there are various ethnic subgroups within the Black community itself. Differences in attitudes, values, life styles, and other cultural patterns exist between southern and northern Blacks, as well as between native-born and immigrant Blacks.

0084. Banks, James A. and Gay, Geneva. "Ethnicity in Contemporary American Society: Toward the Development of a Typology." Ethnicity, Vol. 5, No. 3 (September 1978), pp. 238-251.

> This paper attempts to delineate the basic characteristics of ethnic groups in contemporary U.S. society, and to formulate a typology for defining and classifying ethnic groups. Several types of ethnic groups are identified: cultural, economic, political, eco-political, and holistic. The authors conclude that every American is a member of an ethnic group, and that ethnicity manifests itself in varied forms.

0085. Banton, Michael. Race Relations. New York: Basic Books, 1968. 434 pp.

0086. Barrera, Mario. Race and Class in the Southwest: A Theory of Racial Inequality. Notre Dame: University of Notre Dame Press, 1979. 261 pp.

> This work argues for historical continuities in the system of racial inequality in the Southwest since its conquest by the U.S. The conquest was an expression of a dynamic and expansive American capitalism which called for the displacement of Chicanos from the land. A subordinate labor force was then established, which included Chicanos, Mexicans and other racial minorities. The author uses the concept of a colonial labor force to elucidate the functioning of the exploitative system dominated especially by the mining companies,

railroad companies, and large agricultural concerns. Successive waves of immigrants from Mexico found themselves fitted into a long-established economic and social structure. The last two chapters attempt to formulate a theory of racial inequality which is most similar to the Marxist-structuralist perspective.

0087. Barron, Milton L. "Recent Developments in Minority and Race Relations." The Annals of the American Academy of Political and Social Science, Vol. 420 (July 1975), pp. 125-176.

Reviews the literature on minority and race relations of the period 1968-73. Emphasis is on studies of Black Americans and Black-White relations.

0088. Barth, F., ed. Ethnic Groups and Boundaries: The Social Organization of Culture Difference. Boston: Little, Brown, 1969. 153 pp.

In his now classical introduction to this collection, the anthropologist Barth sets up a new formulation of the concept of ethnicity. Ethnic groups are seen as categories of ascription and identification by social actors themselves. Their primary feature is to organize interaction between people. This interactive and procedural view emphasizes the generating and maintaining of ethnic boundaries. The rest of the book consists of seven ethnographic case studies applying this theoretical framework.

0089. Bernard, William S. "New Directions in Integration and Ethnicity." International Migration Review, Vol. 5, No. 4 (Winter 1971), pp. 464-473.

This article is a summary of the proceedings of the 10th Annual Seminar on the Integration of Immigrants held in 1970. Topics discussed in the seminar include: the idea of the U.S. as "a nation of nations"; assisted integration of new immigrants; Filipino immigrants; and contemporary developments with respect to other immigrants and refugees.

0090. Bernard, William S. Racism, a Worldwide Factor Opposing Migrant Adjustment and How to Combat It. The Hague: Research Group for European Migration Problems, Bulletin Supplement 12, 1978.

0091. Bernard, William S., ed. Immigrants and Ethnicity: Ten Years of Changing Thought. An Analysis Based on the Special Seminars of the American Immigration and Citizenship Conference 1960-1970. New York: American Immigration and Citizenship Conference, 1972. 73 pp.

0092. Berry, Brewton. Race and Ethnic Relations. Boston: Houghton, Mifflin, 1978, 4th edition. 433 pp.

0093. Blauner, Robert. Racial Oppression in America. New York: Harper and Row, 1972. 309 pp.

0094. Broom, L. and Ditsuse, J. I. "The Validation of Acculturation: A Condition of Ethnic Assimilation." American Anthropologist, Vol. 57, No. 1, Part 1 (February 1955) pp. 44-48.

The validation of acculturation is a step taken by an immigrant group after it has acquired the cultural apparatus of the host society. Validation follows access to participation in the dominant institutions. Using Japanese Americans as an example, the authors discuss the ways in which an ethnic community may help or impede the process of validation.

0095. Burgess, M. Elaine. "The Resurgence of Ethnicity: Myth or Reality?" Ethnic and Racial Studies, Vol. 1, No. 3 (July 1978), pp. 265-285.

The meaning of ethnicity is discussed along two axes: rational vs. non-rational characteristics and objective vs. subjective criteria. The contemporary resurgence of ethnicity, though not a totally new phenomenon, reflects the new reality of modern societies. Factors facilitating ethnic resurgence are: (1) expanding role of the polity; (2) erosion of class interests; (3) disintegration of old authority structures; and (4) quest for equality.

0096. Burkey, Richard M. Ethnic and Racial Groups. Menlo Park, CA: Cummings, 1978. 509 pp.

0097. Colburn, D. R. and Pozetta, G. E. America and the New Ethnicity. Port Washington, NY: Kennikat Press, 1979. 243pp.

0098. Cordasco, Francesco M. and Galatioto, Rocco. "Ethnic Displacement in the Interstitial Community: The East Harlem Experience." Phylon, Vol. 31, No. 3 (Fall 1970), pp. 302-312.

This paper traces the movement of the largest ethnic groups through East Harlem, New York City from 1900 to 1960. A pattern of ethnic succession is delineated: Blacks and Italians pushing out Jews while Italians were in turn to be pushed out by Puerto Ricans who in turn would be pushed out by Blacks. The paper concludes with three general points: (1) the importance of ethnicity; (2) the lack of intergroup contact; and (3) the fact that one group will advance at the expense of a group just below it.

0099. Cortes, Carlos E. et al, eds. Three Perspectives on Ethnicity in America: Blacks, Chicanos, and Native Americans. New York: G. P. Putnam's Sons, 1976. 429 pp.

0100. Cox, Oliver C. Caste, Class and Race: A Study in Social Dynamics. New York: Doubleday, 1948. 624 pp. (Reprint, New York: Monthly Review Press, 1970)

0101. Daniels, R. and Kitans, H. H. American Racism. Englewood Cliffs: Prentice-Hall, 1970. 155 pp.

0102. De Vos, George and Romanucci-Ross, Lola, eds. Ethnic Identity. Palo Alto: Mayfield Publishing, 1975. 395 pp. (Second edition, Chicago: University of Chicago Press, 1982)

0103. Dormon, James H. "Ethnic Groups and 'Ethnicity': Some Theoretical Considerations." Journal of Ethnic Studies, Vol. 7, No. 4 (Winter 1980), pp. 23-36.

In this survey of recent literature on ethnicity, the author identifies and attempts to resolve some definitional and conceptual problems.

0104. Engel, M.H. "Ethnic and Racial Groups in Urban Communities in Crisis: A Report of the 8th Annual Seminar on the Integration of Immigrants." International Migration Review, Vol. 2, No. 2 (Spring 1968), pp. 91-95.

The seminar was held on February 15, 1968 at Columbia University. Discussion was highlighted by a repeated emphasis on power as opposed to ethnic culture in the analysis of inter-group relations focusing particularly on groups' needs for a nexus of institutions to insure their relative power position. The seminar also called for new services for current immigrants.

0105. Feagin, Joe R. Racial and Ethnic Relations. Englewood Cliffs: Prentice-Hall, 1978. 392pp.

0106. Francis, E.K. Interethnic Relations: An Essay in Sociological Theory. New York: Elsevier, 1976. 432 pp.

This sociological treatise investigates the meaning of ethnicity and its specific role in various social interaction patterns. It presents ethnographic and historical case studies of the integration of ethnically diverse groups in larger societal units. The largest part of the book is devoted to the discussion of levels and modes of interethnic relations in industrial society. Ethnic relations in colonial situations are also examined with case studies of Sub-Saharan Africa, Mexico, and South Africa.

0107. Friedman, N. L. "Nativism." Phylon, Vol 28 (1967), pp. 408-415.

0108. Fuchs, L. A., ed. American Ethnic Politics. New York: Harper Torchbooks, 1968. 304 pp.

0109. Gelfand, D. E. and Lee, R. D. Ethnic Conflicts and Power: A Cross National Perspective. New York: John Wiley and Sons, 1973. 354 pp.

0110. Glazer, Nathan. "Blacks and Ethnic Groups: The Difference, and the Policital Difference It Makes." Social Problems, Vol 18, No. 4 (Spring 1971), pp. 444-461.

The history of Black development can be analyzed in terms of either the internal colonialism or the White ethnic group model. In the south the internal colonialism model fits the evidence better. However, in the northern cities differences between Black and White ethnic group development are not as sharp as have been suggested, when we examine residential segregation, economic development, and political development. Glazer takes the position that sees Blacks as constituting an ethnic group, seeing them "as the last of the major groups, the worst off, but due to rise over time to larger shares of wealth and power and influence."

0111. Glazer, Nathan. "Politics in a Multiethnic Society." In Ethnic Relations in America. Ed., Lance Liebman. Englewood Cliffs: Prentice-Hall, 1982, pp. 128-149.

Glazer maintains that Blacks and Hispanics have not followed the steps of earlier European immigrants in the quest for equality. He is opposed to affirmative action and government intervention on behalf of ethnic minorities. He counsels for full assimilation of all ethnic and immigrant groups to a common cultural type.

0112. Glazer, Nathan and Moynihan, D. P. Beyond the Melting Pot. Cambridge: The M.I.T. Press. Second Edition, 1970. 363 pp.

0113. Glazer, Nathan and Moynihan, D. P., eds. Ethnicity: Theory and Experience. Cambridge: Harvard University Press, 1975. 531 pp.

0114. Gordon, Milton. Assimilation in American Life: The Role of Race, Religion, and National Origins. New York: Oxford University Press, 1964. 276 pp.

In this classical sociological work, the author formulates a typology of seven stages of the assimilation process. A fundamental distinction is made between cultural and structural assimilation. In American society, despite a massive trend toward cultural assimilation, there have persisted structurally separate subsocieties even in the absence of cultural distinctiveness. Gordon argues that structural pluralism, rather than cultural pluralism, better describes the American situation.

0115. Gordon, Milton. "Models of Pluralism: The New American Dilemma." Annals of the American Academy of Political and Social Science, Vol. 454 (March 1981), pp. 178-188.

0116. Greely, Andrew M. "American Sociology and the Study of Ethnic Immigrant Groups." International Migration Digest, Vol. 1, No. 2 (Fall 1964), pp. 107-113.

Argues that an ethnic collectivity is a bridge between gemeinschaft and geselschaft, between primary and secondary relations. Suggests that, despite the pressures of urbanism and industrialism, certain of the ethnic or nationality groups in American society are still major props of social structure.

0117. Greeley, Andrew M. Ethnicity in the United States. New York: John Wiley & Sons, 1974. 347 pp.

0118. Green, Vera. "Racial versus Ethnic Factors in Afro-American and Afro-Caribbean Migration." In Migration and Development. Eds., H.I. Safa and B.M. DuToit. The Hague: Mouton, 1975, pp. 83-96.

An analysis of data from the United States, Aruba, and Curacao in terms of racial versus ethnic primacy as it obtains in the relationship among migrants. The factors of race and color may be omnipresent in areas with large numbers of persons of African descent, but it is not always the crucial factor. Data from the three cases studied suggest that ethnicity, along with other socioeconomic factors, may act as a mitigating force. The primacy of race, ethnicity, or any other factors depends on the specific situation.

0119. Greer, Colin, ed. Divided Society: The Ethnic Experience in America. New York: Basic Books, 1974. 405 pp.

0120. Handlin, Oscar. Race and Nationality in American Life. Boston: Little, Brown, 1957. 300 pp.

0121. Higham, John, ed. Ethnic Leadership in America. Baltimore: Johns Hopkins University Press, 1978. 214 pp.

0122. Hunt, Chester L. et al. Ethnic Dynamics. New York: Dorsey Press, 1974. 463 pp.

0123. Isaacs, Harold. Idols of the Tribe: Group Identity and Political Change. New York: Harper and Row, 1975. 242 pp.

0124. Kinton, Jack F. American Ethnic Groups and the Revival of Cultural Pluralism. Aurora, IL: Social Science and Sociological Resources, 1974. 206 pp.

0125. Knowles, L. L. and Prewitt, H. K. Institutional Racism in the United States. Englewood Cliffs: Prentice-Hall, 1969.

0126. Kolm, Richard. The Change of Cultural Identity. New York: Arno Press, 1980. 255 pp.

0127. Lambert, Richard D. "Ethnic/Racial Relations in the United States in Comparative Perspective." Annals of the American Academy of the Political and Social Science, Vol. 454 (March 1981), pp. 189-205.

0128. Lee, M. E. and Kramer, M. S. The Ethnic Factor. New York: Simon and Schuster, 1972.

0129. Liebman, Lance. "Ethnic Groups and the Legal System." In Ethnic Relations in America. Ed., Lance Liebman. Englewood Cliffs: Prentice-Hall, 1982, pp. 150-173.

> This article deals first with the issues of groups as legal entities, including their standing to sue, group rights, and representation. It then considers the question of equal protection of the laws. The author concludes that such legal protection is justifiable in the case of Blacks; but as for all other social groupings (women, Hispanics, aliens, etc.), "an attempt to assess and correct guilt is the wrong, and indeed an unconstitutional endeavor."

0130. Liebman, Lance, ed. Ethnic Relations in America. Englewood Cliffs: Prentice-Hall, 1982. 179 pp.

> Contains six background papers for a conference convened by the American Assembly in 1981. All papers are separately annotated in this Bibliography.

0131. McKay, James. "An Exploratory Synthesis of Primordial and Mobilizationist Approaches to Ethnic Phenomena." Ethnic and Racial Studies, Vol. 5, No. 4 (October 1982), pp. 395-420.

> This paper examines the weaknesses and strengths of primordial and mobilizationist approaches to ethnic phenomena. Arguing that the two views are complementary, the author proposes a scattergram or matrix model in order to demonstrate the ways in which the two factors interact in specific situations. A typology of ethnic interests is put forth with illustrations of empirical cases from various parts of the world.

0132. Marshall, Gloria A. (Niara Sudarkasa) "Racial Classifications: Popular and Scientific." In Science and the Concept of Race. Eds., Margaret Mead et al. New York: Columbia University Press, 1968, pp. 149-164.

> A sociopolitical analysis of the use of the race concept and racial classifications. Argues that race has never been a primarily biological concept; rather, both scientific and popular conceptions about race are usually influenced by social, economic, and political considerations.

0133. Mathias, Charles McC., Jr. "Ethnic Groups and Foreign Policy." Foreign Affairs, Vol. 59 (Summer 1981), pp. 975-998.

0134. Miller, Kent S. and Dreger, R. M., eds. Comparative Studies of Black and White in the United States. New York: Seminar Press, 1973. 572 pp.

0135. Mindel, C. H. and Habenstein, R. W. Ethnic Families in America: Patterns and Variations. New York: Elsevier, 1976. 442p.

0136. Moore, Joan W. "Minorities in the American Class System." Daedalus, Vol. 110, No. 2 (Spring 1981), pp. 275-299.

Criticizes the conventional view of the American class system that it eventually provides economic opportunities and upward mobility for all racial and ethnic groups. Argues that the system has worked differently for earlier immigrant groups and for four minorities—Blacks, Native Americans, Chicanos, and Puerto Ricans. Continuing racial discrimination has resulted in the slight improvement for the middle class and the entrenchment of an underclass among these four minorities during the past 20 years.

0137. Mullings, Leith. "The New Ethnicity: Old Wine in New Bottles." Reviews in Anthropology, Vol. 4, No. 4 (November-December 1977), pp. 615-624.

In this critical review of some writings on ethnicity, Mullings emphasizes the determining role of political and economic structure in the emergence and form of ethnicity. She points out the integral relationship between ethnicity and class stratification.

0138. Mullings, Leith. "Ethnicity and Stratification in the Urban United States." The Annals of the New York Academy of Sciences, Vol. 318 (December 1978), pp. 10-22.

After a historical analysis of the unequal structural constraints encountered by different minority groups, the author argues that the term "ethnicity" should not be uncritically applied to all groups. A distinction is made between cultural minorities (e.g., White ethnics) and oppressed minorities (e.g., Afro-Americans). Ethnicity may be usefully applied to all groups only with regard to the ideological-symbolic level. While ethnicity is not analytically reducible to class, at its base is the division of labor and allocation of resources.

0139. Mullings, Leith. "'Tribalism,' Ethnicity, and Group Cohesion." In Group Cohesion. Ed., Henry Kellerman. New York: Grune and Stratton, 1981, pp. 111-119.

The concepts of tribalism and ethnicity have both been misused by social scientists. Neither tribal nor ethnic cohesion is usefully characterized as "primordial," but both can be explained by analysis of social relations. A comparison between Euro-Americans and Afro-Americans reveals that ethnic cohesion and conflict is conditioned by the socio-economic system.

0140. Novak, Michael. The Rise of the Unmeltable Ethnics: The New Political Force of the Seventies. New York: Macmillan, 1971. 321 pp.

0141. Novak, Michael. Further Reflections on Ethnicity. Middletown, PA: Jednota Press, 1977.

0142. Patterson, Orlando. Ethnic Chauvinism: The Reactionary Impulse. New York: Stein and Day, 1977. 347 pp.

The basic premise of this book is that ethnicity is a manifestation of contemporary conservative reaction to the tradition of creative and non-conforming thinking. In part one the author presents a sociohistorical analysis of the origin and development of ethnicity.  He also gives a typology of six major forms of ethnic solidarity.  Part two is an intellectual analysis of the doctrine and ideology of ethnicity put in the context of the traditions of Western social thought.  Ethnic allegiance is seen as a "Hebraic solution" to the crisis of modernity, as industrial civilization has made Jews of us all. Ethnicity as a recommitment in faith is criticized and a "humanistic socialism" is proposed in its stead.

0143.  Pavalko, Ronald M.  "Racism and the New Immigration:  A Reinterpretation of the Assimilation of White Ethnics in American Society."  Sociology and Social Research, VoL 65, No. 1 (October 1980), pp. 56-77.

Points out that the "new immigrants" from eastern, central, and southern Europe were defined as racially inferior and incapable of being assimilated. But once immigration from Europe was effectively restricted, these groups were no longer defined as a threat to racial purity but as a threat to political and economic order.  Argues that this change led to the emphasis on assimilation of the new immigrants.

0144.  Pettigrew, Thomas F.  "Race and Class in the 1980s:  An Interactive View." Daedalus, VoL 110, No. 2 (Spring 1981), pp. 233-255.

Three conventional views on American race relations (the race model, the class-and-caste model, and the social class model) are found to be not only theoretically inadequate, but have been outdated by changing social trends in the past four decades.  These trends include the discontinuities of social change, the class polarization within black America, and the shifting demographic configuration.  As an alternative, the author advocates an interactive model of race and class which emphasizes the joint, interactive effects of the two variables.  This model can better account for the more subtle forms of racism which are currently emerging.

0145.  Polenberg, Richard.  One Nation Divisible:  Class, Race, and Ethnicity in the United States Since 1938.  New York:  Viking Press, 1980.  363 pp.

0146.  Rabkin, Judith G.  Ethnicity, Social Class and Mental Illness:  A Social Area Analysis of Five Ethnic Groups in New York City.  New York: Institute on Pluralism and Group Identity, 1976.

0147.  Rollins, Joan H., ed.  Hidden Minorities:  The Persistence of Ethnicity in American Life.  Washington, DC: University Press of America, 1982.  268 pp.

Includes chapters on Narragansett Indians, Cape Verdeans, Armenians, Syrians, Lebanese, and French Canadians.  Each chapter traces the ethnic group in both its homeland and in American society.  The collection puts forth the thesis that American society represents neither cultural pluralism nor a melting pot; rather, it is a heterogeneous society in which members may share a common system of basic or compulsory institutions, but practice differing alternative and exclusive institutions.

0148.  Roper, Brent S.; Heath, Linda L. and King, Charles D.  "Racial Consciousness:  A New Guise for Traditionalism."  Sociology and Social Research, VoL 62, No. 3 (April 1978), pp. 430-447.

A comparative study of reproductive attitudes and practices among Mexican-Americans, Blacks, and Whites in a Texas city.  The findings suggest that as minorities lose the traditionalism which until now has supported high fertility, it may be replaced by new attitudes of racial consciousness which will still emphasize high fertility.

0149. Rosen, Bernard C. "Race, Ethnicity and the Achievement Syndrome." American Sociological Review, VoL 24, No. 1 (February 1959), pp. 47-60.

This study of six ethnic groups in the Northeast attempts to explain the disparity between their mobility rates as a function of their dissimilar psychological and cultural orientations toward achievement (as defined by McClelland). Data indicate that differences between the groups in motivation, values, and aspirations existed before their arrival in the Northeast, and still exist.

0150. Royce, Anya Peterson. Ethnic Identity: Strategies of Diversity. Bloomington: Indiana University Press, 1982. 247 pp.

0151. Schermerhorn, R.A. Comparative Ethnic Relations: A Framework for Theory and Research. New York: Random House, 1970. (Second edition, Chicago: University of Chicago Press, 1978.) 326 pp.

This sociological work attempts to answer the question: What are the conditions that foster or prevent the integration of ethnic groups into the environing societies? Adopting a system analysis approach, a framework is designed to examine the independent and intervening variables which determine the various modes of integration and conflict.

0152. Schneider, Mark. Ethnicity and Politics. Chapel Hill: Institute for Research in Social Science, University of North Carolina, 1979. 89 pp.

0153. Seda Bonilla, Eduardo. "Who is a Puerto Rican: Problems of Sociocultural Identity in Puerto Rico." Caribbean Studies, VoL 17, No. 1-2 (April-July 1977), pp. 105-121.

In this long review of Soto's novel, Hot Land, Cold Season, the author critiques the pseudo-ethnicity postulated by the American "racistic optic and praxis." True identity should be an exercise in socio-cultural belonging, not a derivative of genetic inheritance. Seda charges that the label "Puerto Rican" is often falsely imposed upon immigrants from the island. He also discusses the predicament of return migrants' search for identity.

0154. Shibutani, I. and Kwan, K. Ethnic Stratification. New York: Macmillan, 1965. 626 pp.

0155. Simpson, G. E. and Yinger, J. M. Racial and Cultural Minorties: An Analysis of Prejudice and Discrimination. New York: Harper and Row, 1973, 4th ed. 777pp.

0156. Smith, Anthony D. The Ethnic Revival in the Modern World. Cambridge: Cambridge University Press, 1981. 240 pp.

The author rejects the economic and cultural explanations of ethnicity. Adopting a socio-historical approach, he argues that the modern form of ethnic revival arose in the 18th century in the West when a historical outlook was pioneered by the intellectuals intent on regenerating historical communities. This ethnic historicism, which identifies private concerns with those of the wider community, was then adopted by the rising professional intelligentsia to legitimate its claims to high status and power in the modern bureaucratic state.

0157. Sowell, Thomas. Race and Economics. New York: David McKay, 1975. 276 pp.

This study of race as a factor in economics starts with an analysis of slavery and its aftermath in the U.S. The economic progress of Blacks is then compared with those of 19th-century immigrants from Europe and 20th-century immigrants from Asia, the Caribbean, and Latin America. Finally, the economics of race is examined in market transactions and in economic activities directed or controlled by the government. The book concludes with some general observations on racial factors in past and future economic life of the U.S.

0158. Sowell, Thomas. "Ethnicity in a Changing America." Daedalus, Vol. 107, No. 1 (Winter 1978), pp. 213-238.

Sowell argues that gross comparisons between ethnic groups are misleading. Interethnic differences in income, occupation, fertility, and attitudes cannot be explained by ethnicity as such. Rather, they are caused by age distribution, geographical distribution, educational disparities, and to a lesser degree, discrimination and government policy.

0159. Sowell, Thomas. Ethnic America: A History. New York: Basic Books, 1981. 353 pp.

In this comparative study, a separate chapter is devoted to each of the following ethnic groups: Irish, Germans, Jews, Italians, Chinese, Japanese, Blacks, Puerto Ricans, and Mexicans. Sowell makes comparisons with regards to a range of demographic and socioeconomic characteristics, and explains the varying success of ethnic groups in the U.S. as resulting from a combination of (1) human capital or the cultural and historical inheritance of an ethnic group, and (2) the social and economic conditions at the time of entry. The author tends to slight the significance of discrimination and bigotry, and argues that all ethnic groups have improved their conditions over time. He concludes by arguing that programs designed to speed up the economic progress of Hispanics and Blacks are dysfunctional and unnecessary.

0160. Sowell, Thomas. Markets and Minorities. New York: Basic books, 1981.

0161. Sowell, Thomas, ed. American Ethnic Groups. Washington, DC: Urban Institute, 1978. 249 pp.

0162. Spiro, M. E. "Acculturation of American Ethnic Groups." American Anthropologist, Vol. 57, No. 1, Part 1 (December 1955), pp. 1240-1252.

This is a survey of anthropological studies of American ethnic groups. The author emphasizes the significance of early childhood experience and pyschological characteristics for the difference in ethnic cultural persistence.

0163. Stein, Howard F. and Hill, Robert F. The Ethnic Imperative: Examining the New White Ethnic Movement. University Park, PA: Pennsylvania State University Press, 1977. 308 pp.

A highly critical analysis of the New Ethnicity. The movement is seen as an ideology reflective of: (1) the illusion of continuity with a hypothetical past; (2) the contemporary cultural ethos and pathos consequent upon the disillusionment with the American Dream; (3) the renewed search for external order and authority; and (4) a cultural pluralism serving to perpetuate the hierarchical structure of American society. The authors propose an alternative "human perspective" which would transcend ethnic categorization and cultural identity.

0164. Steinberg, Stephen. The Ethnic Myth: Race, Ethnicity, and Class in America. New York: Atheneum, 1981. 277 pp.

This book is an attempt at the demystification of ethnicity. The author argues that assimilation has been the reality for immigrant minorities; ironically it is when they have lost their ethnic clutures that ethnic identity is emphasized. The "success" or "failure" of various minority groups is not the result of their cultural values and tradition; rather, it is due to their class position. The author emphasizes class determination of racial and ethnic conflict. Finally, it is argued that since pluralsim as presumed to exist in the U.S. is predicated on inter-group inequality, it is in conflict with the democratic principle.

0165. Tabb, William K. "Race Relations, Models and Social Change." Social Problems, Vol. 18, No. 4 (Spring 1971), pp. 431-444.

This paper compares two models of race relations: (1) the ghetto as internal colony, which draws on a Third World perspective, stressing domination of one racial group by another, and sees independence of the subject people as the goal; (2) Blacks as a marginal working class, which draws on Marxian theory, perceiving the position of Blacks in the U.S. in class terms. Policy implications of the two perspectives are examined.

0166. Taylor, Ronald L. "Black Ethnicity and the Persistence of Ethnogenesis." American Journal of Sociology, Vol. 84, No. 6 (May 1979), pp. 1401-1423.

Earlier writings on Black experience tend to obscure the important role of migration, urbanization, and intergroup conflict in promoting a distinctive Black ethnicity. This study suggests that Black ethnogenesis was determined by essentially the same structural conditions as in the development of ethnic identities and communities among White ethnic populations in American cities.

0167. Teper, S. Ethnicity, Race and Human Development: A Report on the State of Our Knowledge. New York: Institute on Pluralism and Group Identity, 1977. 77 pp.

0168. Te Sella, Sallie. The Rediscovery of Ethnicity. Its Implications for Culture and Politics in America. New York: Harper and Row, 1973. 138 pp.

0169. Thernstrom, Stephan. "Ethnic Groups in American History." In Ethnic Relations in America. Ed., Lance Liebman. Englewood Cliffs: Prentice Hall, 1982, pp. 3-27.

This article attempts to dispel the myth of ethnic revival, especially among ethnic groups of European origin. Assimilation of these groups has proceeded so far that ethnicity has but symbolic meanings. However, other minorities

and Afro-Americans in particular have not fared as well. The author tends
to see this as a matter of time lag, and argues that equality should not be
pursued on the basis of ethnic groups as in affirmative action programs, but
on the basis of persons.

0170. Thernstrom, Stephen, ed. Harvard Encyclopedia of American Ethnic Groups.
Cambridge: Harvard University Press, 1980. 1076 pp.

Contains 29 thematic essays on various aspects of immigration and ethnicity,
as well as articles on over 100 ethnic groups. Selections from the Encyclopedia are later republished in several volumes on specific topics.

0171. van den Berghe, Pierre L.  Race and Racism: A Comparative Perspective.
New York: Wiley, 1967. 169 pp.

0172. van den Berghe, Pierre L.  Race and Ethnicity: Essays in Comparative
Sociology. New York: Basic Books, 1970. 312 pp.

0173. van den Berghe, Pierre L.  The Ethnic Phenomenon.  New York: Elsevier,
1981. 301 pp.

0174. Weaver, Robert C.  "The Impact of Ethnicity upon Urban America." In
Ethnic Relations in America.  Ed., Lance Liebman.  Englewood Cliffs: Prentice-
Hall, 1982, pp. 66-100.

This article begins with an analysis of the roles of ethnic groups in U.S.
economy.  It then describes recent changes in the ethnic composition of
urban residential pattern and politics.  While urban areas continue to deterio-
rate, ethnic minorities are trapped in ghettos of poverty.  The city no longer
functions for them as a gateway to assimilation and equality, as it did for
European immigrants.  Finally, the author advocates coalitions beyond ethnic
boundaries.

0175. Wilson, William Julius.  The Declining Significance of Race.  Chicago:
University of Chicago Press, 1978.  Second expanded edition, 1980. 243 pp.

This book relates the transformation of American economy and polity to its
class and racial systems.  Three stages of American race relations are delineated: (1) a first period of plantation economy and racial-caste oppression;
(2) late 19th century to the end of the New Deal era, the period of industrial
expansion, class conflict, and racial oppression; and (3) the post-WWII era,
marked by a progressive transition from racial inequalities to class inequalities.  The thrust of the book's argument is that today a segmented labor
market leads to decreasing job opportunities for the Black lower class, while
the Black middle class is enjoying unprecedented success in finding jobs in
the corporate and government sectors.  On the basis of this observation,
Wilson asserts that the increasing importance of class also signifies the
decreasing importance of race.

0176. Wilson, William Julius.  "The Black Community in the 1980s: Questions of
Race, Class, and Public Policy." Annals of the American Academy of Political
and Social Science, Vol. 454 (March 1981), pp. 26-41.

0177. Yancey, William L.; Ericksen, Eugene P. and Juliani, Richard N.  "Emergent
Ethnicity: A Review and Reformulation." American Sociological Review, Vol.
41, No. 3 (July 1976), pp. 391-403.

This paper argues against the view that cultural heritage is the defining characteristic of ethnicity; rather, it may be better explained by the relationship of ethnic community to the larger society--particularly the constraints of occupation, residence, and institutional affiliation.

0178. Yinger, J. Milton. "Recent Developments in Minority and Race Relations." The Annals of the American Academy of Political and Social Science, VoL 378 (July 1968), pp. 130-145.

Reviews the literature on minority and race relations of the period 1963-68. Four areas of scholarly research are discussed: (1) the social psychology of prejudice and discrimination; (2) pluralism; (3) minority and race relations in major institutions; and (4) the civil rights movement.

0179. Zenner, Walter P. "Ethnic Assimilation and Corporate Group." Sociological Quarterly, VoL 8, No. 3 (Summer 1967), pp. 340-348.

This paper applies the distinction between corporate and noncorporate group to the process of ethnic assimilation. It is found that, in case of corporate ethnic groupings, assimilation tends to take the radical form of "conversion" or "passing", while in case of noncorporate ethnic groups, assimilation is gradual.

# III.
# U. S. Immigration
# Legislation and Policies

0180. Allen, Gary. "Illegal Aliens." American Opinion, VoL 21 (January 1978), pp. 33-54.

0181. American Enterprise Institute for Public Policy Research. Illegal Aliens. Washington, DC, 1978. 37 pp.

0182. Appleman, I. "That New Immigration Act: Changes That Were Made in the Nation's Immigration Policy by the Passage Last Year of a New Immigration and Nationality Act." American Bar Association Journal, VoL 52 (August 1966), pp. 717-722.

0183. Benn, D. "The New U.S.A. Immigration Law." International Migration, VoL 3 (1965), pp. 99-110.

0184. Bennett, M. "The Immigration and Nationality Act of 1952, as Amended to 1965." Annals of the American Academy of Political and Social Science, VoL 367 (September 1966), pp. 127-136.

0185. Bernard, William S. "Refugee Asylum in the United States: How the Law Was Changed to Admit Displaced Persons." International Migration, VoL 13, No. 1/2 (1975), pp. 3-20.

0186. Boyd, Monica. "Immigration Policies and Trends: A Comparison of Canada and the United States." Demography, VoL 13 (1976), pp. 83-104.

   Outlines the similarities and differences between the two countries' immigration policies. Both countries emphasize labor needs and the desirability of
   reuniting families. Canada emphasizes job preparation and uses immigration
   as a part of its economic programs. The United States is more restrictive in
   its immigration policies, and assigns most of its immigrant quotas to family
   members.

0187. Bracamonte, Jose A. "The Carter Immigration Bill: A Critical Analysis." Journal of Legislation, VoL 5 (1979), pp. 107-120.

0188. Briggs, Vernon M., Jr. "The Problem of Illegal Immigration." Texas Business Review, VoL 51 (August 1977), pp. 171-175.

0189. Briggs, Vernon M., Jr. Foreign Labor Programs as an Alternative to Illegal Immigration Into the United States: A Dissenting View. College Park: Center for Philosophy and Public Policy, University of Maryland, 1980. 32 pp.

0190. Butler, Broadus N. "Humanity, U.S. Immigration and Refugee Policy, and the Select Commission." The Crisis, Vol. 88, No. 10 (December 1981), pp. 497-503.

0191. Carter, Hugh, ed. "Reappraising Our Immigration Policy." Annals of the American Academy of Political and Social Science, Vol. 262 (March, 1949), pp. 1-92.

> Volume includes twenty-one articles dealing with four general topics: (1) historical aspects of immigration; (2) demographic factors in immigration policy; (3) assimilation of the foreign born; and (4) current immigration problems in the United States.

0192. Castillo, Kionel J. "Legislative and Judicial Developments: Dealing with the Undocumented Alien - An Interim Approach." International Migration Review, Vol. 12, No. 4 (Winter 1978), pp. 570-577.

0193. Chiswick, Barry R., ed. The Gateway: U.S. Immigration Issues and Policies. Washington, DC: American Enterprise Institute for Public Policy Research, 1982. 476 pp.

> This volume contains the proceedings of a conference on "U.S. Immigration Issues and Policies" held in 1980. Papers are grouped into four parts: (1) the supply of and demand for immigrants; (2) the progress of immigrants; (3) the economic impact of immigrants; and (4) alternative immigration policies. Selected papers are separately listed in this Bibliography.

0194. Cordi, Thomas D. et al. The Report of the U.S. Select Commission on Immigration and Refugee Policy: A Critical Analysis. Program in U.S.-Mexican Studies Working Paper No. 32, University of California, San Diego.

0195. Cornelius, Wayne A. Illegal Migration to the United States: Recent Research Findings, Policy Implication and Research Priorities. Cambridge: Center for International Studies, MIT, 1977. 28 pp.

0196. Cornelius, Wayne A. "The Reagan Administration's Proposals for a New U.S. Immigration Policy: An Assessment of Potential Effects." International Migration Review, Vol. 15, No. 4 (Winter 1981), pp. 769-778.

0197. Donohue, John W. "The Uneasy Immigration Debate." America, Vol. 145 (March 20, 1982), pp. 206-209.

0198. Fitzhugh, David. "The Silent Invasion." Foreign Service Journal, Vol. 53 (January 1976), pp. 7-10, 26.

0199. Fogel, Walter A. "Major Changes to Control Immigration Flow." Center Magazine, Vol. 10 (March 1977), pp. 46-47.

0200. Fogel, Walter A. "Illegal Aliens: Economic Aspects and Public Policy Alternatives." San Diego Law Review, Vol. 15 (December 1977), pp. 63-78.

0201. Fogel, Walter A. "United States Immigration Policy and Unsanctioned Migrants." Industrial and Labor Relations Review, VoL 33, No. 3 (April 1980), pp. 295-311.

0202. Fragomen, Austin T., Jr. "1976 Amendments to the Immigration and Nationality Act." International Migration Review, VoL 11, No. 1 (Spring 1977), pp. 95-100.

0203. Fragomen, Austin T., Jr. "President Carter's Amnesty and Sanctions Proposal." International Migration Review, VoL 11, No. 4 (Winter 1977), pp. 524-532.

0204. Fragomen, Austin T., Jr. "New Asylum Regulations - Legislative and Judicial Developments." International Migration Review, VoL 13, No. 2, (Summer 1979), pp. 347-351.

0205. Fragomen, Austin T., Jr. "The Immigration and Nationality Act. Part I -International Personnel: Legislative and Judicial Developments." International Migration Review, VoL 14, No. 1 (Spring 1980), pp. 116-123.

0206. Fragomen, Austin T., Jr. "The Final Report and Recommendations of the Select Commission on Immigration and Refugee Policy: A Summary." International Migration Review, VoL 15, No. 4 (Winter 1981), pp. 758-768.

0207. Fragomen, Austin T., Jr. "Immigration and Nationality Act of 1981." International Migration Review, VoL 16, No. 1 (Spring 1982), pp. 206-222.

0208. Friedman, S. "The Effect of the U.S. Immigration Act of 1965 on the Flow of Skilled Migrants from Less Developed Countries." World Development, VoL 1 (August 1973), pp. 39-44.

0209. "General Assistance for Education of Cuban and Haitian Refugees." Congressional Record Daily, VoL 126 (September 25, 1980): S13492-S13499.

0210. Gerking, Shelby D. "Costs and Benefits of Illegal Immigration: Key Issues for Government Policy." Social Science Quarterly, VoL 61 (June 1980), pp. 71-85.

0211. Gerking, Shelby D. and Mutti, John H. Illegal Immigration: Economic Consequences for the United States. Denver: Westview Press, 1982. 130 pp.

0212. Gordon, Wendell. "The Problem of Illegal Aliens." Texas Business Review, VoL 51 (August 1977), pp. 167-170.

0213. Graebner, H. A. "Roots of Our Immigration Policy." Current History, VoL 29 (November 1955), pp. 285-292.

0214. Graham, Otis L., Jr. "Illegal Immigration: The Problem That Will Not Go Away." Center Magazine, VoL 10, No. 4 (July-August 1977), pp. 56-66.

Criticizes the ineffectiveness of government policies concerning illegal aliens. Argues that illegal immigration should be curtailed because it inflicts upon the U.S. economy enormous social welfare costs and has undesirable impacts on its population size.

0215. Graham, Otis L., Jr. "Illegal Immigration and the New Restrictionism, with reply by V. Villalpando." Center Magazine, VoL 12 (May 1979), pp. 54-64.

The author advocates immigration restriction on two grounds: (1) the need for population stabilization; (2) to improve the labor market, especially the bottom sector.

0216. Graham, Otis L., Jr. "The New Immigration: An Exchange. Illegal Immigration and the Left." Dissent, Vol. 27 (Summer 1980), pp. 341-346.

Advocates the restriction of immigration on two grounds: (1) the influx of immigrants undermines the urgent task of stabilizing U.S. population size; (2) immigrants displace natives from job market and their presence results in a general depression of wages and standards of living.

0217. Griffith, Elwin. "The Alien Meets Some Constitutional Hurdles in Employment, Education, and Programs." San Diego Law Review, Vol. 17 (March 1980), pp. 201-231.

0218. Harthy, W. "United States Immigration Policy: The Case of the Western Hemisphere." World Affairs, Vol. 135 (Summer 1972), pp. 54-70.

0219. Hewlett, Sylvia Ann. "Coping with Illegal Immigrants." Foreign Affairs, Vol. 60, No. 2 (Winter 1981-82), pp. 358-378.

This article proposes a four-point program to reduce and control the flow of illegal immigrants. The four policy measures are: (1) employer sanctions; (2) worker identification; (3) control of borders; and (4) an amnesty program. Immigration policy proposals of the Reagan Administration are evaluated.

0220. Higham, John. "American Immigration Policy in Historical Perspective." Law and Contemporary Problems, Vol. 21 (Spring 1956), pp. 213-235.

0221. Hutchinson, E.P. Legislative History of American Immigration Policy, 1798-1965. Philadelphia: University of Pennsylvania Press, 1978. 685 pp.

This book presents a chronological account of all bills dealing with aliens and of Congressional deliberations on them from 1798 to 1965. The author analyzes the development of uniform national immigration policies as opposed to differing state laws related to the regulation of alien entry. Criteria used by Federal regulations to restrict alien entry are discussed.

0222. Hutchinson, E., ed. "The New Immigration." Annals of the American Academy of Political and Social Science, Vol. 367 (September 1966), pp. 1-149.

Fourteen papers dealing with the historical background and implications of the 1965 U.S. Immigration Act. They are grouped under three sections: (1) Characteristics of the new immigration; (2) Administration of the immigration laws; and (3) Recent legislative action.

0223. "Immigration Symposium." San Diego Law Review, Vol. 14 (December 1976), whole issue.

0224. Jacobs, James B. "Aliens in the U.S. Armed Forces: A Historical-Legal Analysis." Armed Forces and Society, Vol. 7 (Winter 1981), pp. 187-208.

0225. Jaeger, G. "Refugee Asylum: Policy and Legislative Developments." International Migration Review, Vol. 15 (Spring/Summer 1981), pp. 52-68.

0226.  Keely, Charles B.  "The Immigration Act of 1965: A Study of the Relationship of Social Science Theory to Group Interest and Legislation."  Ph.D.  dissertation, Fordham University, 1970. (DAI: 31/05A, p. 2513)

0227.  Keely, Charles B.  "Effects of the Immigration Act of 1965 on Selected Population Characteristics of Immigrants to the United States."  Demography, Vol. 8, No.
2 (May 1971), pp. 157-169.

   The 1965 Act led to changes in the origins of immigrants.  Southern European,
   Asian and Caribbean immigrants made up a larger proportion of immigrants
   than previously.  After the Act, the sources of the various occupational groups
   shifted to some extent.  It also led to an increase in the number of female
   household workers from Mexico and the Caribbean.

0228.  Keely, Charles B.  "Effects of U.S. Immigration Law on Manpower Characteristics of Immigrants."  Demography, Vol. 12 (1975), pp. 179-191.

   Examines the effects of the 1965 U.S. Immigration Law: (1) it opened up
   immigration to countries where the interest was greater; (2) it changed the
   occupational composition of the immigrants, increasing the blue-collar segment; (3) it increased the use of status adjustment by immigrants.

0229.  Keely, Charles B.  "Development of U.S. Immigration Policy Since 1965."
Journal of International Affairs, Vol. 33, No. 2 (Fall/Winter 1979), pp. 249-263.

0230.  Keely, Charles B.  U.S. Immigration: A Policy Analysis.  New York: The
Population Council, 1979.  87 pp.

0231.  Keely, Charles B.  "Illegal Migration."  Scientific American, Vol. 246, No. 3
(March 1982), pp. 41-47.

   Argues that the effects of illegal migrants are not uniformly harmful; the
   U.S. economy as a whole probably does not suffer from their presence.  On
   the other thand, the non-economic aspects of illegal migration, specificially
   its illegality, are very disturbing to U.S. society.  Immigrants denied the protection of the law and rendered vulnerable by their illegal status threaten the
   integrity of U.S. society.

0232.  Keely, Charles B.  "Immigration and the American Future."  In Ethnic Relations in America.  Ed., Lance Liebman.  Englewood Cliffs: Prentice-Hall, 1982, pp.
28-65.

   This article first gives a history of the U.S. immigration policy between 1952-
   1980.  It then examines the major issues underlying policy debates and options,
   including: the impact of immigration on population growth, the immigration
   selection criteria, the refugee issue, the issue of worker migration, and the
   regional distributional effects of immigration.

0233.  Kennedy, E.  "The Immigration Act of 1965."  Annals of the American Academy
of Political and Social Science, Vol. 367 (September 1966), pp. 137-149.

0234.  Kennedy, E. M.  "Refugee Act of 1980."  International Migration Review,
Vol. 15 (Spring/Summer 1981), pp. 141-156.

0235.  Knight, Franklin W.  "Who Needs a Guest-Worker Program?  They Do and We
Do."  Caribbean Review, Vol. 11, No. 1 (Winter 1982), pp. 46-47, 64.

Advocates the institution of a guest-worker program in the U.S. patterned after the European system. The author argues that such legalizing and regularizing of status serves the interests of both migrant workers and the U.S. economy. It also offers benefits for the U.S. and the sending countries.

0236. Krajick, Kevin. "Refugees Adrift: Barred from America's Shores." Saturday Review, Vol. 6 (October 27, 1979), pp. 17-20.

0237. Kurth, J. R. "Refugees: America Must Do More." Foreign Policy, No. 36 (Fall 1979), pp. 12-19.

0238. Lehman, H. "Towards a New Immigration Policy." Journal of International Affairs, Vol. 7 (1953), pp. 86-92.

0239. Levi, David F. "The Equal Treatment of Aliens: Preemption or Equal Protection?" Stanford Law Review, Vol. 31 (July 1979), pp. 1069-1091.

0240. Levine, Barry B. "Surplus Populations: Economic Migrants and Political Refugees." Caribbean Review, Vol. 11, No. 1 (Winter 1982), pp. 4-5.

The human dramas involved in migration--whether for economic or political reasons--are always the same: migrants are defenseless and rightless, but they are also full of hope and courage. Immigration policy should be based on this recognition.

0241. McCarthy, Kevin F. and Ronfeldt, David F. U.S. Immigration Policy and Global Interdependence. Santa Monica, CA: Rand Corporation, 1982. 17 pp.

Argues that immigration should be regarded as part of a "global flow," not as a strictly internal matter. Immigration policies should not just serve the immediate interests of the U.S., but have to take into account long-term economic and foreign policy considerations.

0242. McClellan, Grant S., ed. Immigrants, Refugees, and U.S. Policy. New York: H.W. Wilson, 1981. 195 pp.

0243. McCoy, Terry L. "A Primer for U.S. Policy on Caribbean Emigration." Caribbean Review, Vol. 8, No. 1 (January-March 1979), pp. 10-15.

Argues that the U.S. immigration policies encourage illegal immigration from the Caribbean.

0244. Marshall, Ray. "Guest Workers: No Need, No Justification." American Federationist, Vol. 88 (August 1981), pp. 15-19.

0245. Martin, Philip L. "Illegal Immigration: The Guestworker Option." Public Policy, Vol. 28 (Spring 1980), pp. 207-229.

0246. Martin, Philip L. "Select Commission Suggests Changes in Immigration Policy--A Review Essay." Monthly Labor Review, Vol. 185 (February 1982), pp. 31-37.

0247. Martin, Philip L. and Miller, Mark J. "Guestworkers: Lessons from Western Europe." Industrial and Labor Relations Review, Vol. 33, No. 3 (April 1980), pp. 315-330.

This article appraises the guestworkers programs of Western Europe and presents several reservations on the proposal to adopt a similar program in the
United States.

0248. Masanz, Sharon D. "Recent Haitian Immigration to the United States."
Congressional Research Service, Education and Public Welfare Division, 1981.

0249. Midgley, Elizabeth. "Immigrants: Whose Huddled Masses?" Atlantic, VoL
241 (April 1978), pp. 6, 9-12, 18, 20, 26.

0250. Miller, Tim. "Sharp Differences on Immigration Law Changes Could Doom a
Bill This Year." National Journal, VoL 14 (February 20, 1982), pp. 336-338.

0251. Moore, Charlotte. "Refugees in the United States: The Cuban Emigration
Crisis." Congressional Research Service, Education and Public Welfare Division,
1981.

0252. National Council on Employment Policy. Illegal Aliens: An Assessment of
the Issues. A Policy Statement and Conference Report with Background Papers.
Washington, DC, 1976. 76 pp.

0253. North, David S. "Illegal Aliens: Fictions and Facts." Worklife, VoL 2
(December 1977), pp. 17-18, 20-21.

0254. North, David S. "The Non-sense of Immigration and Welfare Policies." Public
Welfare, VoL 40 (Winter 1982), pp. 29-35.

0255. Peirce, Neal R. "Should the United States Open Its Doors to the Foreigners
Waiting to Come In?" National Journal, VoL 13 (March 7, 1981), pp. 390-393.

0256. Piore, MichaeL "The 'New Immigration' and the Presumptions of Social
Policy." Proceedings of the 27th Annual Meeting, Industrial Relations Research
Association, 1975, pp. 350-358.

0257. Piore, MichaeL "The 'Illegal Aliens' Debate Misses the Boat." Working Papers
for a New Society, VoL 6 (March-April 1978), pp. 60-69.

Argues that people come to the U.S. because of labor needs. Immigrants
come to take the low-status jobs rejected by native workers. Without recog-
nizing this fact immigration legislation reform will only worsen the situation.

0258. Piore, MichaeL "The New Immigration: An Exchange. Another View on
Migrant Workers." Dissent, VoL 27 (Summer 1980), pp. 346-351.

This is a critique of Otis L. Graham's (q.v.) article. Piore argues that the
cause of international migration is not economic differentials or population
pressures per se, but rather the result of explicit recruitment efforts by
American employers or their agents. The restriction of immigration will not
enhance job opportunities for native workers. A policy attempting at limiting
immigration is inconsistent with the social and political realities of American
life.

0259. Reimers, David M. "Post-World War II Immigration to the United States:
America's Latest Newcomers." Annals of the American Academy of Political and
Social Science, VoL 454 (March 1981), pp. 1-12.

Traces the changes in post-1945 United States immigration laws and their implications. Immigrants coming after 1945 were more likely to be refugees and to have higher skill levels than before. The majority were females.

0260. Reimers, David M. "Recent Immigration Policy: An Analysis." In The Gateway: U.S. Immigration Issues and Policies. Ed., Barry R. Chiswick. Washington, DC: American Enterprise Institute for Public Policy Research, 1982, pp. 13-53.

A detailed historical analysis of the post - 1940 liberalization of immigration policy. It examines how foreign policy, ethnic politics, religious agencies, and economic issues have influenced the formulation of immigration policy, especially as regards the question of national origins quotas.

0261. Reubens, Edwin P. "Aliens, Jobs, and Immigration Policy." Public Interest, No. 51 (Spring 1978), pp. 113-134.

0262. Reubens, Edwin P. Immigration Problems, Limited-Visa Programs, and Other Options. College Park: Center for Philosophy and Public Policy, University of Maryland, 1980. 49 pp.

0263. Rivera, Mario. The Cuban and Haitian Influxes of 1980 and the American Response: Retrospect and Prospect. Washington, DC: Cuban Haitian Task Force, 1980.

0264. Robbins, R. H. The Immigration Act of 1952: A Case Study in Political Sociology. Ann Arbor: University of Michigan Microfilms, 1959.

0265. Rockett, Ian R.H. "American Immigration Policy and Ethnic Selection: An Historical Overview." Journal of Ethnic Studies, Vol. 10, No. 4 (Winter 1983), pp. 1-26.

With respect to ethnic selection, the history of U.S. immigration policy has been much more reactive than prospective. Although the 1965 Immigration Act attempts to introduce equity on the ethnic score, the problem of ethnic selection persists. As regards to illegal immigration, there is little ground for thinking that the problem will be legislated away in the short term.

0266. Rodino, P "New Immigration Law in Retrospect." International Migration Review, Vol. 2, No. 3 (Summer 1968), pp. 56-61.

0267. Rogers, R. "Charter for Immigrant Children." New Statesmen, Vol. 98, No. 496 (October 5, 1979).

0268. Rosenberg, John S. "The Chaos of Immigration Policy." The Nation, Vol. 227, No. 6 (September 2, 1978), pp. 174-176, 178.

Current debates on immigration policy show the lingering influence of cold-war ideology of the Truman-McCarthy era.

0269. Rudnick, E. "The Immigration and Naturalization and Citizenship Laws." International Migration Review, Vol. 5 (Winter 1971), pp. 420-435.

0270. Sofer, Eugene F. Illegal Immigration: Background to the Current Debate. Washington, DC: CONEG Policy Research Center, 1980.

0271. Stang, A. "Immigration." American Opinion, Vol. 22 (January 1979), pp. 11-12, 14-15, 17, 19-20, 101, 103-105, 107-108.

0272. Stewart, Teresa M. "Illegal Immigration: Employer Sanctions and Related Proposals." San Diego Law Review, VoL 19 (December 1981), pp. 149-176.

0273. Taft, Julia V.; North, David S. and Ford, David A. Refugee Resettlement in the U.S.: Time for a New Focus. Washington, DC: New Trans Century Foundation, 1979. 222 pp.

0274. Teitelbaum, M. S. "Right vs. Right: Immigration and Refugee Policy in the United States." Foreign Affairs, VoL 59 (Fall 1980), pp. 21-59.

0275. Thomas, J. "Cuban Refugee Program." Welfare in Review, VoL 1 (September 1963), pp. 1-28.

0276. United Nations Association of the U.S.A. Immigration Policy PaneL Illegal Immigration: Challenge to the United States. New York, 1981. 68 pp.

0277. U.S. Commission on Civil Rights. The Tarnished Golden Door: Civil Rights Issues in Immigration. Washington, DC: U.S. Government Printing Office, 1980. 158 pp. (SuDoc Number: CR1.2:T17)

0278. U.S. Congress. House Committee on Education and Labor. Subcommittee on Elementary, Secondary, and Vocational Education. The Alien Education Impact Aid Act of 1981. Hearings, 97th Congress, 1st Session. Washington, DC: U.S. Government Printing Office, 1982. 65 pp. (SuDoc Number: Y4.Ed8/1:A14/3)

0279. U.S. Congress. House Committee on the Judiciary. Subcommittee on Immigration, Citizenship, and International Law. Haitian Emigration. 94th Congress, 2nd Session. Washington, DC: U.S. Government Printing Office, 1976. 36 pp. (SuDoc Number: Y4.J89/1:412/2)

0280. U.S. Congress. House Committee on the Judiciary. Subcommittee on Immigration, Citizenship, and International Law. Illegal Aliens. Washington, DC: U.S. Government Printing Office, 1975. 450 pp. (SuDoc Number: Y4.J89/1:94-8)

0281. U.S. Congress. House Committee on the Judiciary. Subcommittee on Immigration, Citizenship, and International Law. Oversight of INS Policies and Legal Issues. Hearings, 95th Congress, 2nd Session, August 3, 1978. Washington, DC: U.S. Government Printing Office, 1979. (SuDoc Number: Y4.J89/1:95/59)

0282. U.S. Congress. House Committee on the Judiciary. Subcommittee on Immigration, Refugees, and International Law. Caribbean Migration. Hearings, 96th Congress, 2nd Session, May 13, June 4, 17, 1980. Washington, DC: U.S. Government Printing Office, 1980. 313 pp. (SuDoc Number: Y4.J89/1:96/84)

0283. U.S. Congress. House Committee on the Judiciary. Subcommittee on Immigration, Refugees, and International Law. Immigration Reform. Hearings, 97th Congress, 1st Session, Part 1. Washington, DC: U.S. Government Printing Office, 1982. 762 pp. (SuDoc Number: Y4.J89/1:97/30/pt.1)

0284. U.S. Congress. House Committee on the Judiciary. Subcommittee on Immigration, Refugees, and International Law. Immigration Reform. Hearings, 97th Congress, 1st Session, Part 2. Washington, DC: U.S. Government Printing Office, 1982. 1360 pp. (SuDoc Number: Y4.J89/1:97/30/pt.2)

0285. U.S. Congress. House Committee on International Relations. Subcommittee on Inter-American Affairs. Undocumented Workers: Implications for U.S. Policy in the Western Hemisphere. Hearings, 95th Congress, 2nd Session. Washington, DC: U.S. Government Printing Office, 1978. 473 pp. (SuDoc Number: Y4.In8/16:W89)

0286. U.S. Congress. House Committee on the Judiciary. Virgin Islands Nonimmigrant Alien Adjustment Act of 1981. Washington, DC: U.S. Government Printing Office, 1981. 17 pp. (SuDoc Number: Y1.1/8:97-307)

0287. U.S. Congress. House Committee on the Judiciary. Subcommittee No. 1. Illegal Aliens. Hearings, 92nd Congress. Washington, DC: U.S. Government Printing Office, 1973. 85 pp. (SuDoc Number: Y4.J89/1:93-(nos.))

0288. U.S. Congress. House Committee on the Judiciary. Subcommittee No. 1. Illegal Aliens. A review of hearings conducted during the 92nd Congress. Washington, DC: U.S. Government Printing Office, 1973. 27 pp. (SuDoc Number: Y4.J89/1:A14/6)

0289. U.S. Congress. House Select Committee on Population. Legal and Illegal Immigration to the United States. Report, 95th Congress, 2nd Session. Washington, DC: U.S. Government Printing Office, 1978. 68 pp. (SuDoc Number: Y4.P81:95/c)

0290. U.S. Congress. Senate Committee on the Judiciary. Caribbean Refugee Crisis: Cubans and Haitians. Hearings, 96th Congress, 2nd Session. May 12, 1980. Washington, DC: U.S. Government Printing Office, 1980. 288 pp. (SuDoc Number: Y4.J89/2:96-58)

0291. U.S. Congress. Senate Committee on the Judiciary. The Refugee Act of 1979 Hearings, 96th Congress, 1st Session, March 14, 1979. Washington, DC: U. S. Government Printing Office, 1979. 396 pp. (SuDoc Number: Y4.J89/2:96-1)

0292. U.S. Congress. House Committee on Foreign Affairs. The Refugee Act of 1979. Hearings, 96th Congress, 1st Session, September 19 and 25, 1979. Washington, DC: U.S. Government Printing Office, 1979. 99 pp. (SuDoc Number: Y4.F76/1:R25/2)

0293. U.S. Congress. Senate Committee on the Judiciary. U.S. Refugee Programs, 1981. Hearings, 96th Congress, 2nd Session. September 19, 1980. Washington, DC: U.S. Government Printing Office, 1980. 288 pp. (SuDoc Number: Y4.J89/2:96-79)

0294. U.S. Congress. Senate Committee on the Judiciary. The World Refugee Crisis: The International Community's Response. A Report Prepared by the Congressional Research Service, 96th Congress, 1st Session. Washington, DC: U.S. Government Printing Office, 1979. (SuDoc Number: Y4.J89/2:R25/18)

0295. U.S. Congress. Senate Committee on the Judiciary. Subcommittee on Immigration and Naturalization. Immigration 1976. Hearings, 94th Congress, 2nd Session. Washington, DC: U.S. Government Printing Office, 1976. 274 pp. (SuDoc Number: Y4.J89/2:Im6/3/976)

0296. U.S. Congress. Senate Committee on the Judiciary. Subcommittee on Immigration and Refugee Policy. Final Report of the Select Commission on Immigration and Refugee Policy. Washington, DC: U.S. Government Printing Office, 1981. 784 pp. (SuDoc Number: Y4.J89/1:Im6/11)

0297. U.S. Congress. Senate Select Committee on Small Business. The Effects of Proposed Legislation Prohibiting the Employment of Illegal Aliens on Small Business. Hearings, 94th Congress, 2nd Session, Nov. 22-23, 1976. Washington, DC: U.S. Government Printing Office, 1977. 380 pp. (SuDoc Number: Y4.Sm1/2:L52)

0298. U.S. Department of Justice. Office of the Attorney General. Illegal Immigration: President's Program. Washington, DC, 1978. 30 pp.

0299. U.S. Department of State. Cuban-Haitian Task Force. A Report of the Cuban-Haitian Task Force. Washington, DC, 1980. 116 pp.

0300. U.S. General Accounting Office. Illegal Aliens: Estimating Their Impact on the United States. Washington, DC: U.S. Government Printing Office, 1980. 128 pp. (SuDoc Number: GA1.13:PAD-80-22)

0301. U.S. General Accounting Office. Number of Undocumented Aliens Residing in the United States Unknown. Washington, DC, 1981. 3 pp. (SuDoc Number: GA1.13:GGD-81-56)

0302. U.S. Library of Congress. Congressional Research Service. Illegal Aliens and Alien Labor: A Bibliography and Compilation of Background Materials. Washington, DC: U.S. Government Printing Office, 1977. 58 pp. (SuDoc Number: Y4.J89/1:AL4/8)

0303. U.S. Library of Congress. Congressional Research Service. U.S. Immigration Law and Policy: 1952-1979. Washington, DC: U.S. Government Printing Office, 1979. 109 pp. (SuDoc Number: Y4.J89/2:Im6/4/952-79)

0304. U.S. Library of Congress. Congressional Research Service. Temporary Worker Programs: Background and Issues. Washington, DC: U.S. Government Printing Office, 1980. 144 pp. (SuDoc Number: Y4.J89/2:W89/3)

0305. U.S. Library of Congress. Education and Public Welfare Division. Illegal Aliens: Analysis and Background. Washington, DC: U.S. Government Printing Office, 1977. 73 pp.

0306. U.S. Select Commission on Immigration and Refugee Policy. U.S. Immigration Policy and the National Interest. Washington, DC, 1981. 453 pp. (SuDoc Number: Y3.Im6/2:2Im6/981)

0307. Vialet, Joyce C. The West Indies Temporary Alien Labor Program: 1943-1977. A Study Prepared for the Subcommittee on Immigration of the Committee on the Judiciary, United States Senate. Washington, DC: U.S. Government Printing Office, 1978. 44 pp.

0308. Viviano, Frank. "The New Immigrants." Mother Jones, Vol. 8, No. 1 (January 1983), pp. 26-33, 45-46.

This article emphasizes the political ambivalence and ideological splits among recent immigrants from Asia and the Caribbean basin. Frictions over immigration policy are also examined.

0309. Wachter, Michael L. "Second Thoughts about Illegal Immigrants." Fortune (May 22, 1978), pp. 80-87.

Illegal immigrants play a useful role in the U.S. economy. In the future their presence may be welcome. Specifically, they could rescue the Social Security system. There is no indication that the U.S. government is prepared to seriously limit illegal immigration.

0310. Weber, Arnold B. "The Role of the Department of Labor in Immigration." International Migration Review, Vol. 4 (Summer 1970), pp. 31-46.

0311.  Weinberg, R. D.  Eligibility for Entry to the U.S.A.  New York:  Oceana Publications, 1967.

0312.  Wenk, Michael G.  "The Alien Adjustment and Employment Act of 1977:  A Summary."  International Migration Review, Vol. 11, No. 4 (Winter 1977), pp. 533-538.

# IV.
# Aspects of Black Immigration

# 1.
# General History of Black Immigration

0313. Katznelson, I. Black Men, White Cities: Race, Politics, and Migration in the United States, 1900-1930, and Britain, 1948-1968. New York: Oxford University Press, 1973. 219 pp.

0314. Reid, Ira de Augustine. The Negro Immigrant: His Background, Characteristics and Social Adjustments, 1899-1937. New York: Columbia University Press, 1939. Reprinted, New York: Arno Press, 1969. 261 pp.

> This classical study focuses on Black immigrants from the Caribbean, particularly the British West Indies. It begins with a brief account of the historical and social background of the Caribbean region. The immigrant populations are described in terms of various demographic characteristics. The bulk of the book is a detailed analysis of the adjustment of immigrants, paying particular attention to the relationship between immigrant and native-born Blacks. The author discusses three factors in this relationship: the low visibility of Black immigrants; their different tradition; and competition between the two groups. Various aspects of immigrant adjustment are discussed, including customs, marriage, religious practice, folklore, and political organization. The book includes several life histories of immigrants. The thrust of Reid's argument is that Black immigrants have a record of considerable achievements in the U.S., although not without price. Despite conflict and antagonism between the two groups, the presence of Black immigrants has broadened the social vision of the native Black group, fostered unity, and accelerated inter-racial progress.

0315. Reid, Ira de Augustine. "The Negro Immigrant." In When Peoples Meet: A Study in Race and Culture Contacts. Alain Locke and B. J. Stein, eds. New York: Hinds, Hayden and Eldridge, 1946, pp. 582-590.

# 2.
# Demography and Settlement Patterns

0316. Aguirre, B.E.; Schwirian, Kent P. and La Greca, Anthony J. "The Residential Patterning of Latin American and Other Ethnic Populations in Metropolitan Miami." Latin American Research Review, Vol. 15, No. 2 (1980), pp. 35-63.

Using 1970 census data this study analyzes ethnic residential patterning in Miami in terms of three ecological dimensions: centralization, segregation, and dissimilarity. Cubans and Puerto Ricans are found to be the most centralized groups. The degree of centralization cannot be explained by these groups' socioeconomic status. On the other hand, these and other groups' patterns of residential segregation and dissimilarity seem to be a function of the groups' status composition, while other variables, such as self-selectivity and enforced constraint in housing choice, also enter into residential distribution differences. In general, the residential patterning is similar to that of European ethnic groups in earlier times.

0317. Baroni, Geno. Who's Left in the Neighborhood? A Report on Relative Conditions in the White, Black and Hispanic Working Class Neighborhoods of Our Older Industrial Cities. Washington, DC: U.S. Office of Minority Business Enterprise, 1976. 47 pp.

0318. Bean, Frank D. and Frisbie, W. Parker, eds. The Demography of Racial and Ethnic Groups. New York: Academic Press, 1978. 321 pp.

0319. Bresnick, David. "Blacks, Hispanics, and Others: Decentralization and Ethnic Succession." Urban Education, Vol. 12 (July 1977), pp. 129-152.

0320. Burman, J. Spanish-Speaking Groups in the United States. Durham, NC: Duke University Press, 1954.

0321. Campbell, Gibson. "The Contribution of Immigration to the U.S. Population Growth: 1790-1970." International Migration Review, Vol. 9 (1975), pp. 157-177.

Estimates that net immigration to the U.S. between 1790 and 1970 amounted to 35.5 million persons.

0322. Fitzpatrick, J.P. and Parker, Lourdes Travieso. "Hispanic-Americans in the Eastern United States." Annals of the American Academy of Political and Social Science, Vol. 454 (March 1981), pp. 98-110.

0323. Glen, Maxwell. "Illegal Aliens Issue May Complicate Census Count of Minority Groups." National Journal, Vol. 12 (January 26, 1980), pp. 144-145.

0324. Greenwood, Michael J. and McDowell, John M. "The Supply of Immigrants to the United States." In The Gateway: U.S. Immigration Issues and Policies. Ed., Barry R. Chiswick. Washington, DC: American Enterprise Institute for Public Policy Research, 1982, pp. 55-85.

This econometric study shows that actual immigration to the U.S. is substantially less than would be predicted by a theoretical model. U.S. immigration laws are an impediment to the free flow of immigrants. The study then examines the major determinants of immigration rates. These include: distance; earnings differentials; level of development of the sending country; and the ability of prospective immigrants to transfer their occupational knowledge to the U.S. labor market.

0325. Gurak, Douglas T. "Sources of Ethnic Fertility Differences: An Examination of Five Minority Groups." Social Science Quarterly, Vol. 59 (September 1978), pp. 295-310.

0326. Hardin, Garret. "Population and Immigration: Compassion or Responsibility?" Ecologist, Vol. 7 (August-September 1977), pp. 268-272.

0327. Huss, John D. "Illegal Immigration: The Hidden Population Bomb." Futurist, Vol. 11 (April 1977), pp. 114-118, 120-124.

0328. Jasso, Guillermina and Rosenzweig, Mark R. "Estimating the Emigration Rates of Legal Immigrants Using Administrative and Survey Data: The 1971 Cohort of Immigrants to the United States." Demography, Vol. 19, No. 3 (August 1982), pp. 279.

This study provides estimates of the cumulative rates of emigration from the U.S. between 1971 and 1979 among several immigrant groups. Emigration rate among Canadian immigrants was probably between 51 and 55 percent. Emigration rates for legal immigrants from Central America, the Caribbean (excluding Cuba), and South America were between 50 and 70 percent. Emigration rates for Koreans and Chinese could not have exceeded 22 percent over the same period.

0329. Kantrowitz, Nathan. Ethnic and Racial Segregation in the New York Metropolis: Residential Patterns Among White Ethnic Groups, Blacks, and Puerto Ricans. New York: Praeger, 1973. 104 pp.

A statistical study of the patterns of residential segregation in New York City, based on the 1960 census. Findings indicate that ethnic and racial forces are the determinants of residential segregation. Within each ethnic or racial group, socioeconomic differentials further segregate the rich from the poor.

0330. Keely, Charles B. "Counting and the Uncountable: Estimates of Undocumented Aliens in the U.S." Population and Development Review, Vol. 3, No. 4 (December 1977), pp. 473-481.

This article discusses the sources of difficulty in making accurate estimates of the flow and stock of undocumented aliens in the U.S. and reviews recent estimates. It concludes that the estimates have been weak, and that they are guided by budget needs and organizational dynamics, rather than by a concern for reliable counts and careful estimation techniques.

0331. Keely, Charles B. "The Shadows of Invisible People." American Demographics, Vol. 2 (March 1980), pp. 24, 26-29.

0332. Keely, Charles B. and Kraly, Ellen P. "Recent Net Alien Immigration to the United States: Its Impact on Population Growth and Native Fertility." Demography, Vol. 15, No. 3 (August 1978), pp. 267-283.

The authors argue that the level of recent net alien immigration is lower than is assumed in the literature. This lower estimate level diminishes the amount of projected population growth due to immigration. The authors' lower estimates also require a smaller reduction in native fertility for maintaining a stationary U.S. population.

0333. McAlister, Ronald J. "The Distribution of the Foreign Stock Population in Selected Metropolitan Areas: 1970." Sociology and Social Research, Vol. 62 (January 1978), pp. 212-227.

0334. Massey, Douglas S. "Residential Segregation of Spanish Americans in United States Urbanized Areas." Demography, Vol. 16, No. 4 (November 1979), pp. 553-563.

Residential segregation among Spanish Americans, Whites, and Blacks is measured in the 29 largest U.S. urbanized areas as of the 1970 Census. The degree of Spanish segregation from Whites is much less than that of Blacks from Whites, and it shows a more pronounced decline between central cities and suburbs. Spanish Americans are also much less concentrated within central cities. Spanish segregation from Whites is found to decline with successive generations in the U.S., but the same does not hold for Blacks.

0335. Massey, Douglas S. "Hispanic Residential Segregation: A Comparison of Mexicans, Cubans, and Puerto Ricans." Sociology and Social Research, Vol. 65, No. 3 (April 1981), pp. 311-322.

This paper examines patterns of residential segregation among the three Hispanic groups in eight U.S. urbanized areas. With the exception of Puerto Ricans of the Northeast, these groups tend to be highly segregated from Blacks, and less segregated from non-Hispanic Whites. They also tend to be considerably less concentrated within central cities than Blacks, with the exception of Puerto Ricans in New York and Chicago. Finally, the three Hispanic groups display a rather high degree of segregation among themselves.

0336. Moynihan, Daniel P. "Patterns of Ethnic Succession: Blacks and Hispanics in New York City." Political Science Quarterly, Vol. 94 (Spring 1979), pp. 1-14.

0337. Nicholas, J.D. and Prohias, Rafael J. Rent Differentials Among Racial and Ethnic Groups in Miami. Boca Raton: Florida Atlantic University—Florida International University Joint Center for Environmental and Urban Problems, 1973.

A study of housing discrimination in various types of neighborhoods in Miami. The groups considered include:  Blacks, Whites, Black Cubans, and White Cubans.

0338.  Platt, Kathleen S.  "Hispanic Americans."  American Demographics, Vol. 1 (January 1979), pp. 40-41.

0339.  Ropka, Gerald W.  The Evolving Residential Patterns of Mexican, Puerto Rican, and Cuban Population in the City of Chicago.  New York: Arno Press, 1980.

0340.  Ross, Elmer L.  Factors in Residence Patterns Among Latin Americans in New Orleans, Louisiana:  A Study in Urban Anthropological Methodology.  New York: Arno Press, 1980.

0341.  Schnare, Ann B.  "Trends in Residential Segregation by Race: 1960-1970." Journal of Urban Economics, Vol. 7 (May 1980), pp. 293-301.

0342.  Sehgal, Ellen and Vialet, Joyce.  "Documenting the Undocumented Data, Like Aliens, Are Elusive."  Monthly Labor Review, Vol. 103, No. 10 (October 1980), pp. 18-21.

Reviews some recent estimates of the undocumented alien population in the U.S.  The lack of valid information has hampered the efforts to estimate their economic and societal impact.

0343.  Siegel, J.S.; Passel, J.S. and Robinson, J.G.  "Preliminary Review of Existing Studies of the Number of Illegal Residents in the United States."  In U.S.  Immigration Policy and the National Interest, The Staff Report of the Select Committee on Immigration and Refugee Policy.  Appendix E:  Papers on Illegal Immigration to the U.S., 1980.

0344.  U.S. Bureau of Census.  Persons of Spanish Origin in the United States: March 1975.  Washington, DC: U.S. Government Printing Office, 1976.  62 pp. (SuDoc Number: C56.21P:P-20/280)

0345.  Wareing, J.  "The Changing Pattern of Immigration into the United States, 1956-1975."  Geography, Vol. 63, No. 3 (July 1978), pp. 220-224.

0346.  Warren, Robert.  "Recent Immigration and Current Data Collection." Monthly Labor Review, Vol. 100, No. 10 (October 1977), pp. 36-41.

This article highlights recent trends in immigration and emigration, and briefly examines some of the demographic characteristics of recent immigrants.  The deficiencies of immigration data are pointed out.

# 3.
# Employment and Economics

0347. Anderson, Bernard E. and Cottingham, Phoebe H. "The Elusive Quest for Economic Equality." Daedalus, Vol. 110, No. 2 (Spring 1981), pp. 257-275.

Reviews the progress in employment and economic position between 1950 and 1980 of four minority groups: Native Americans, Blacks, Mexican Americans, and mainland Puerto Ricans. Overall, the gap among these minority groups is smaller than that between them and Whites. The greatest gains in minority occupational positions occurred during the 1960s, while the 1970s saw a slowing down of progress. The most plausible explanation of the limited minority economic improvement is labor market discrimination. Government policies for reducing economic inequalities are discussed.

0348. Bonacich, Edna. "A Theory of Ethnic Antagonism: The Split Labor Market." American Sociological Review, Vol. 37, No. 5 (October 1972), pp. 547-559.

0349. Borjas, George J. "The Earnings of Male Hispanic Immigrants in the United States." Industrial and Labor Relations Review, Vol. 53, No. 3 (April 1982), pp. 343-353.

This paper analyzes the earnings differential among male immigrants of various Hispanic groups. The most important finding is that the rate of economic progress of Cuban immigrants exceeds that of other Hispanic groups. This results in part from the fact that Cuban immigrants have invested more heavily in U.S. schooling. The author concludes that political refugees are likely to face higher costs of return migration and hence have greater incentives to adapt rapidly to the U.S. labor market.

0350. Boyd, Monica. "Occupations of Female Immigrants and North-American Immigration Statistics." International Migration Review, Vol. 10 (1976), pp. 73-80.

0351. Briggs, V. M., Jr. "Illegal Immigration and the American Labor Force: The Use of Soft Data for Analysis." American Behavioral Scientist, Vol. 19, No. 3 (January-February 1976), pp. 351-363.

Despite the "softness" and sometimes questionable nature of the data on immigration, social scientists still must be engaged in the careful assessment

of critical social issues involved in immigration. The author proposes sub-
stitute information to supplement and to check official statistics. He argues
that illegal aliens do have negative effects upon regional and local labor
market, and the problems are getting worse.

0352. Burawoy, Michael. "The Functions and Reproduction of Migrant Labor:
Comparative Material from Southern Africa and the United States." American
Journal of Sociology, Vol. 81, No. 5 (October 1976), pp. 1050-1087.

0353. Bustamente, Jorge. "Structural and Ideological Conditions of the Mexican
Undocumented Immigration to the United States." American Behavioral Scientist,
Vol. 19, No. 3 (January-February, 1976), pp. 364-376.

This article focuses upon the conditions in which social policies related to
Mexican immigration are inextricably linked to a class-structured society.
Adopting a Marxian perspective, the author exposes the myth that causally
attributes high unemployment to immigration to the U.S. The myth has
served to fragment workers and protect the interests of dominant groups.

0354. Chiswick, Barry R. "Immigrant Earnings Patterns by Sex, Race and Ethnic
Groupings." Monthly Labor Review, Vol. 103, No. 10 (October 1980), pp. 22-25.

Based on 1970 Census data, this study indicates that most immigrant men
reach earnings equality with the native born in 11 to 15 years; for women,
earnings following arrival vary more by racial and ethnic groups; skills and
motive for migrating significantly affect economic performance.

0355. Chiswick, Barry R. "Immigrants in the U.S. Labor Market" Annals of the
American Academy of Political and Social Science, Vol. 460 (March 1982), pp.
64-72.

This paper focuses on immigrants of the past 15 years. Overall, adult male
immigrants earn about the same as native-born males, but important
differences among the foreign born are attributed to duration of residence,
reason for migrating, and country of origin. Immigrant earnings rise with
increased length of U.S. residence. Economic migrants reach earnings equality
with the native born when they have been in the U.S. for about 11-15 years.
Refugees have lower earnings than other categories of immigrants.

0356. Chiswick, Barry R. "The Economic Progress of Immigrants: Some Apparently
Universal Patterns." In The Gateway: U.S. Immigration Issues and Policies. Ed.
Barry R. Chiswick. Washington, DC: American Enterprise Institute for Public
Policy Research, 1982, pp. 110-158.

This paper presents the same findings as in the preceeding entry. It goes on
to show that those earnings patterns are also found among immigrants in
four other settings: the U.S. at the turn of the century, contemporary Canada,
Great Britain, and Israel.

0357. DeFreitas, Gregory E. "What Is the Occupational Mobility of Black
Immigrants?" Monthly Labor Review, Vol. 104, No. 4 (April 1981), pp. 44-45.

This study indicates that Black immigrants experience significant downward
occupational mobility during their first few years following arrival in the
U.S.

0358. Dixon, Marlene; Jonas, Susanne and McCaughan, Ed. "Reindustrialization and the Transnational Labor Force in the United States Today." Contemporary Marxism, No. 5 (Summer 1982), pp. 101-115.

Today the U.S. is facing a period of capitalist crisis. Three effects of this crisis are examined: (1) Relocation of industries in the Third World in order to take advantages of cheap labor force; (2) employment of immigrant labor and the creation of a vulnerable labor force; and (3) reindustrialization based on the superexploitation of a transnational working class.

0359. Ellison, Julian. "The New York City Fiscal Crisis and Its Economic Impact on Minority Communities." Review of Black Political Economy, Vol. 6 (Spring 1976), pp. 331-341.

0360. Freeman, Gary P. Immigrant Labor and Racial Conflict in Industrial Societies. Princeton: Princeton University Press, 1979. 362 pp.

0361. Gupta, Udayan. "From Other Shores." Black Enterprise, Vol. 13, No. 8 (March 1983), pp. 51-54.

Describes the strained relationship between Blacks and new immigrants, especially in business and job market. Also points out that in reality Black Americans have not been displaced by immigrants.

0362. Hill, H. "Tragedy of the Florida Farm Worker." The Crisis, Vol. 70, No. 10 (December 1963), pp. 596-601.

This is the author's testimony before a U.S. Department of Labor hearing. Hill highlights the continuing deterioration of the working and living conditions of migratory farm laborers. He points out that 14,000 Black workers in Florida were displaced by West Indian immigrants.

0363. Hill, Peter J. The Economic Impact of Immigration into the United States. New York: Arno Press, 1975. 130 pp.

0364. Jackson, Jacquelyne J. "Illegal Aliens: Big Threat to Black Workers." Ebony, Vol. 34, No. 6 (April 1979), pp. 33-36, 38, 40.

The siphoning of jobs by the large number of illegal aliens is a major reason for the unemployment crisis among Blacks, especially young Black men. The author advocates outlawing the employment of illegal aliens.

0365. Jaco, Daniel E.; Hagan, Robert J. and Wilber, George L. Spanish Americans in the Labor Market. Lexington: University of Kentucky Press, 1974.

0366. Jenkins, J. Craig. "The Demand for Immigrant Workers: Labor Scarcity or Social Control?" International Migration Review, Vol. 12, No. 4 (Winter 1978), pp. 514-535.

Reviews two interpretations of the economic role of immigrant workers from Mexico in U.S. labor market—the labor scarcity argument and the social control thesis. The former interpretation is challenged. In support of the social control thesis, it is argued that immigrants are recruited by employers to displace domestic workers, and thus lower wages.

0367. Jimenez, Dave and Smith, David Lionel. "Illegal Aliens: Another View –
Surviving in a Racist System." Ebony, Vol. 34, No. 11 (September 1979), pp. 93–94,
96, 98.

Argues that the contention that undocumented workers are parasites and that
they take jobs away from U.S. citizens are both false. Like Blacks, they are
the victims of racism and forced to live under the worst conditions.

0368. Johnson, George. E. "The Labor Market Effects of Immigration." Industrial
and Labor Relations Review, Vol. 33, No. 3 (April 1980), pp. 331–341.

This paper argues that a high rate of immigration is likely to have a big impact
on the distribution of income in the U.S. The most important impact is on
the wage rates of low-skilled labor rather than on the employment of low-
skilled native workers. Immigration also raises the earnings of high-skilled
workers and capital owners.

0369. Johnson, Ralph. "Are Illegal Aliens to Blame for Black Unemployment."
Sepia, Vol. 26, No. 4 (April 1977), pp. 18–24.

A small but vocal group of Brooklyn Blacks see illegal immigration as a basic
cause of Black joblessness. Their leader considers these aliens as "vermin, a
virus that must be eradicated if we are to witness the very survival of our
people." Also contains personal testimonies of some Haitians in Brooklyn.
These Haitians do not assimilate well with native Blacks.

0370. Katzman, Martin. "Opportunity, Subculture, and the Economic Performance
of Urban Ethnic Groups." American Journal of Economics and Sociology, Vol. 28,
No. 4 (October, 1969), pp. 351–366.

Through a regression analysis of 1950 U.S. Census data for 14 ethnic groups
living in the nation's nine largest metropolitan areas (12 European and Canadian
ethnic groups, and Mexicans and Puerto Ricans), this study finds that ethnic
factors—nationality and nativity—as well as ethnic differences in marital,
educational, and labor force status account for a considerable proportion of
the variance in occupational structure, income, unemployment, and labor
force participation.

0371. Katzman, Martin T. "Urban Racial Minorities and Immigrant Groups: Some
Economic Comparisons." The American Journal of Economics, Vol. 30, No. 1 (January
1971), pp. 15–256.

Compares the economic performance of six racial groups: Blacks, Mexicans,
Puerto Ricans, Chinese, Filipinos, and Japanese. Among them the Blacks and
Mexican Americans are found to have the lowest economic achievement.
This under-achievement cannot be explained solely by prejudice, but must
also be explained in terms of sub-cultural traits such as attitudes towards
work, saving, education, and fertility.

0372. Levering, R. "Is Business Pro or Con Illegal Immigration?" Business and
Society Review, No. 24 (Winter 1977–1978), pp. 55–59.

0373. Lewis, S. G. Slave Trade Today. American Exploitation of Illegal Aliens.
Boston: Beacon Press, 1979. 239 pp.

0374. Light, I. H. Ethnic Enterprise in America: Business and Welfare among
Chinese, Japanese and Blacks. Berkeley: University of California Press, 1972.

0375. McAvoy, T. T. "Success of Later Immigrants." <u>Social Order</u>, Vol. 12 (January 1962), pp. 1-12.

0376. McPheters, Lee R. "Macroeconomic Determinants of the Flow of Undocumented Aliens in North America." <u>Growth and Change</u>, Vol. 12 (January 1981), pp. 2-8.

0377. Martin, Philip L. and Richards, Alan. "International Migration of Labor: Boon or Bane?" <u>Monthly Labor Review</u>, Vol. 103, No. 10 (October 1980), pp. 4-9.

Contrary to the expectation of trade theory, recent flows of international labor migration have not provided economic benefits to workers, employers and societies. The undesired results of international labor migration are unemployment and low wages for native workers and employer addiction to low-cost labor.

0378. Martinez, V. S. "Illegal Immigration and the Labor Force: A Historical and Legal View." <u>American Behavioral Scientist</u>, Vol. 19, No. 3 (January-February 1976), pp. 335-350.

Reviews the history of Mexican immigration in the 20th century. On the basis of historical analysis, the article proceeds to discuss the relation between public policy and the rights of minority groups. It concludes that "successful" policies designed to remove illegal aliens from the labor force neglect their fundamental rights.

0379. Miller, Mark J. and Boyer, William W. "Foreign Workers in the USVI: History of a Dilemma." <u>Caribbean Review</u>, Vol. 11, No. 1 (Winter 1982), pp. 48-51.

Describes the administration of the USVI temporary worker program. The labor shortages in the USVI were caused by employer preferences for alien workers. It was employers who profited the most from the H-2 program. The dilemma of the alien workers resulted from their temporary legal status while being employed permanently. The program has long divorced the alien as an economic agent from his/her social existence.

0380. Montoya, Alfredo C. "Hispanic Workforce: Growth and Inequality." <u>AFL-CIO American Federationist</u>, Vol. 86 (April 1979), pp. 8-11.

0381. Newman, Morris J. "A Profile of Hispanics in the U.S. Work Force." <u>Monthly Labor Review</u>, Vol. 101, No. 12 (December, 1978), pp. 3-14.

This article examines the labor force patterns of the major Hispanic ethnic groups: Mexican, Cuban, Puerto Rican and others. Considerable variation among these groups exists in virtually all employment-related characteristics; divergent age distributions have a strong effect on labor force participation.

0382. North American Congress on Latin America. "Undocumented Immigrant Workers in New York City." <u>NACLA Latin America and Empire Report</u>, Vol. 12, No. 6 (1979).

0383. North, David S. <u>Seven Years Later: The Experiences of the 1970 Cohort of Immigrants in the U. S. Labor Market</u>. Washington, DC: Linton and Co., Inc. in Cooperation with Center for Labor and Migration Studies, New Trans Century Foundation and Trans-Century Corp., 1978. 124 pp.

0384. North, David S. "Nonimmigrant Workers: Visiting Labor Force Participants." <u>Monthly Labor Review</u>, Vol. 103, No. 10 (October 1980), pp. 26-30.

Nonimmigrant workers include students, temporary workers, and professionals. This article discusses the labor market characteristics of the several categories of nonimmigrant workers.

0385. North, David S. and Houstoun, Marion F. The Characteristics and Role of Illegal Aliens in the U.S. Labor Market: An Exploratory Study. Washington, DC: Linton, 1976.

0386. North, David S. and Martin, Philip L. "Immigration and Employment: A Need for Policy Coordination." Monthly Labor Review, Vol. 103, No. 10 (October 1980), pp. 47-50.

In coming years, immigrants may constitute as much as 45 percent of U.S. labor-force growth. Efforts are needed to ensure that national goals for immigration and employment are complementary.

0387. Orton, Eliot S. "Changes in the Skill Differential: Union Wages in Construction, 1970-1972." Industrial and Labor Relations Review, Vol. 30 (1976), pp. 16-24.

Evaluates the effect of illegal immigration on wages. Shows that illegal immigrants depressed the wages of unskilled workers in the 1960s and widened the gap between the earnings of skilled and unskilled workers.

0388. Parlin, Bradley W. "Immigrants, Employers, and Exclusion." Transaction/-Society, Vol. 14, No. 6 (September/October 1977), pp. 23-26.

Discusses employment restrictions encountered by immigrants, especially immigrant professionals. An analysis of the socio-legal environment reveals a pattern of employment discrimination against noncitizen immigrant professionals. Recent changes in U.S. immigration policies and Supreme Court decisions tend to encourage this discrimination.

0389. Piore, Michael J. "Impact of Immigration on the Labor Force." Monthly Labor Review, Vol. 98, No. 5 (May 1975), pp. 41-44.

Based on a study of Puerto Rican migration to Boston, this article argues that new immigrants are recruited by employers for positions at the bottom of job hierarchy which are eschewed by native workers.

0390. Piore, Michael J. "Immigration, Work Experience and Labor Market Structure." In The Diverse Society: Implications for Social Policy. Eds., Pastora San Juan Cafferty and Leon Chestang. Washington, DC: National Association of Social Workers, 1976, pp. 109-128.

0391. Portes, Alejandro. "Labor Functions of Illegal Aliens." Transaction/Society, Vol. 14, No. 6 (September/October 1977), pp. 31-38.

Using Mexican immigrants as an example, Portes argues that the fundamental cause underlying illegal migration has to do with the contemporary operations, needs, and constraints of the developed capitalist economy. Illegal immigration serves to maintain rates of profit by increasing the flexibility of exploitation of labor, and through the vulnerability and defenselessness of immigrant workers.

0392. Portes, Alejandro and Walton, J. Labor, Class, and the International System. New York: Academic Press, 1981.

0393. Richmond, Anthony, H. and Verma, Ravi P. "The Economic Adaptation of Immigrants: A New Theoretical Perspective." International Migration Review, Vol. 12, No. 1 (Spring 1978), pp. 3-38.

Argues that immigrant adaptation must be understood in a multi-variate context in which economic factors are only one dimension. Both classical "functionalist" and neo-Marxist theories of migration are found inadequate to explain international trends of migration and the Canadian experience of immigration since WW II. As an alternative, the authors put forward a "global systems model" of international and internal migration. The implications of the different theoretical perspectives for the economic adaptation of immigrants are discussed.

0394. Rios, Palmira N. "Evaluating a Work Incentive Program: Report on Employability Services for Hispanic Women." In Female Immigrants to the United States. Eds., D.M. Mortimer and R.S. Bryce-Laporte. Washington, DC: Smithsonian Institution, Research Institute on Immigration and Ethnic Studies, Occasional Papers No. 2, 1981, pp. 267-295.

0395. Rochin, Refugio I. "Illegal Aliens in Agriculture: Some Theoretical Considerations." Labor Law Journal, Vol. 29 (March 1978), pp. 149-167.

0396. Ross, Stanley R. and Weintraub, Sidney. "Temporary" Alien Workers in the United States. Boulder: Westview Press, 1982. 124 pp.

0397. Safa, Helen I. "The Differential Incorporation of Hispanic Women Migrants into the United States Labor Force." In Female Immigrants to the United States. Eds., D.M. Mortimer and R.S. Bryce-Laporte. Washington, DC: Smithsonian Institution, Research Institute on Immigration and Ethnic Studies, Occasional Papers No. 2, 1981, pp. 235-266.

0398. Sassen-Koob, Saskia. "The International Circulation of Resources and Development: The Case of Migrant Labor." Development and Change, Vol. 9 (1978), pp. 509-545.

0399. Sassen-Koob, Saskia. "Immigrant and Minority Workers in the Organization of the Labor Process." Journal of Ethnic Studies, Vol. 8, No. 1 (Spring 1980), pp. 1-34.

This paper examines the conditions that produce and reproduce low-wage labor supply, and the mechanism of labor market fragmentation which organizes the different categories of labor. Immigrant and native minority workers are overrepresented in low wage jobs in the secondary labor market sector. In a general sense they can be viewed as functional equivalents. However, because of the powerlessness of immigrant workers, they are preferred by employers as a cheaper source of labor. This leads to the displacement of native workers, and contributes to the conflict between the two groups of low-wage workers.

0400. Sassen-Koob, Saskia. "The Internationalization of the Labor Force." Studies in Comparative International Development, Vol. 15, No. 4 (Winter 1980), pp. 3-25.

This paper first describes the conditions under which labor imports have historically been an important factor in the constitution of labor supply. It then examines the labor supply function and the cost lowering and anticyclical effects of labor imports in three major contemporary cases: the oil exporting countries, Western Europe, and the United States.

0401. Sassen-Koob, Saskia. "Exporting Capital and Importing Labor: The Role of Women." In Female Immigrants to the United States. Eds., D.M. Mortimer and R.S. Bryce-Laporte. Washington, DC: Smithsonian Institution, Research Institute on Immigration and Ethnic Studies, Occasional Papers No. 2, 1981, pp. 203-234.

0402. Sassen-Koob, Saskia. "Towards a Conceptualization of Immigrant Labor." Social Problems, Vol. 29, No. 1 (October 1981), pp. 65-85.

The consolidation of the world economic system is the condition for the emergence of migrations as a labor-supply system. At the same time, the formation of modern nation-states creates the conditions for immigrant labor as a distinct category in the labor process. The article discusses the growing presence of immigrant labor in the tertiary sector of all core countries and its relationship to the export of manufacturing plants to the periphery.

0403. Sassen-Koob, Saskia. "Recomposition and Peripheralization at the Core." Contemporary Marxism, No. 5 (Summer 1982), pp. 88-100.

Labor migrations since the middle 1960s are closely associated with the world-wide recomposition of capital. The case of New York City is used for elaboration of the argument. From 1960 to 1980 the city's economy was restructured to intensify its highly specialized service industries at the expense of manufacturing sectors. The large influx of immigrant workers provides cheap labor for the jobs that serve the growth industries. It is the recomposition process, not the influx of immigrants per se, that has caused the displacement of certain segments of native labor force.

0404. Stewart, James B. and Hyclak, Thomas. "Ethnicity and Economic Opportunity." American Journal of Economics and Sociology, Vol. 38, No. 3 (July 1979), pp. 319-335.

Argues that human capital alone (as contended by Thomas Sowell among others) cannot account for variations in economic performance. Through a statistical analysis of the 1970 Census data, this paper supports the hypothesis that economic discrimination against particular ethnic groups has been and continues to be an important force generating differential economic performance.

0405. Szymanski, Albert. "The Growing Role of Spanish Speaking Workers in the U.S. Economy." Aztlan, Vol. 9 (Spring-Fall 1978), pp. 177-208.

This article examines the trend in which Spanish speaking immigrants are replacing Blacks in various categories of menial and low-paying jobs, while the latter have acquired industrial skills and are in a better position to resist oppression. Detailed comparisons of these two groups with respect to labor force participation, occupational position, and income are given. It includes case studies of Blacks and Spanish speaking people in New York and California.

0406. Wachter, Michael. "The Labor Market and Illegal Immigration: The Outlook for the 1980s." Industrial and Labor Relations Review, Vol. 33, No. 3 (April 1980), pp. 342-354.

This article attempts to isolate those occupations and age-sex groups that are likely to have a shortfall of workers and to match the characteristics of these categories with the demographic characteristics of illegal alien work force. The author predicts a shortage of unskilled workers which will be met by an increased flow of immigrants. This flow of immigrants will benefit skilled workers and owners of capital, but harm domestic unskilled workers.

0407.  Wilbur, George et al.  Spanish Americans and Indians in the Labor Market.
Lexington: University of Kentucky Press, 1975.

# 4.
# Education, Health, and Social Services

0408. Alvarez, Rodolfo, ed. <u>Delivery of Services for Latino Community Mental Health</u>. Los Angeles: University of California, 1975. 80 pp.

0409. Berkowitz, Rhoda H. and Divorkie, M. <u>The Impact of Puerto Rican Migration on Governmental Services in New York City</u>. New York: New York University Press, 1957.

0410. Cohen, Lucy M. <u>Culture, Disease, and Stress among Latino Immigrants</u>. Washington, DC: Smithsonian Institution, Research Institute on Immigration and Ethnic Studies, Special Study, 1979. 314 pp.

0411. Duran, D.L. <u>Latino Communication Patterns</u>. New York: Arno Press, 1980. 508 pp.

> This is a study of the communication behavior patterns of Mexican, Cuban, and Puerto Rican residents of Chicago. It examines the relationships between these variables: membership in voluntary associations, interpersonal communication, use of media resources, use of primary group resources, and use of information agencies.

0412. Freudenberger, H.J. "Dynamics and Treatment of the Young Drug Abuser in an Hispanic Therapeutic Community." <u>Journal of Psychedelic Drugs</u>, Vol. 7 (July 1975), pp. 273-280.

0413. Harwood, Alan, ed. <u>Ethnicity and Medical Care</u>. Cambridge: Harvard University Press, 1981. 509 pp.

> Contains six anthropological case studies (urban Blacks, Chinese, Haitians, Mexican-Americans, Navahos, and Puerto Ricans). Each chapter deals with the group's medical beliefs, disease patterns, and ways of coping with illness.

0414. Laughlin, M.A. "An Invisible Minority: An Examination of Migrant Education." <u>Explorations in Ethnic Studies</u>, Vol. 4, No. 1 (January 1981), pp. 50-59.

0415. Malzberg, Benjamin. "Mental Disease among Native and Foreign Born Negroes in New York State." <u>Journal of Negro Education</u>, Vol. 25 (Spring 1965), pp. 175-181.

0416. Mooney, M. C. "Immigration and Colonial Models of Police-Community Relations: An Inquiry." Journal of Police Science and Administration, Vol. 6 (July 1978), pp. 622-631.

0417. Naditch, M. P. and Morrissey, R. F. "Role Stress, Personality, and Psychopathology in a Group of Immigrant Adolescents." Journal of Abnormal Psychology, Vol. 85, No. 1 (February 1976), pp. 113-118.

A role-stress-personality framework was applied to the analysis of psychopathological symptoms in a nonclinical sample of 155 Cuban refugees in Miami. Results suggest that high rates of mental illness among immigrants may be partially a function of evaluation ambiguity and the resultant problems of identity formation amid conflicting cultural patterns.

0418. Seller, M. S. Ethnic Communities and Education in Buffalo, New York: Politics, Power, and Group Identity, 1838-1979. Buffalo: State University of New York, 1979. 136 pp.

0419. Susser, Ida and Glick, Nina. "Ethnicity in a New York City School." Student Anthropologist, Vol. 3 (1970), pp. 133-142.

0420. Zimmer, Richard. Use of Church and Community Support Services Among Catholic and Protestant Latino Congregations. Sonoma State College.

Latino immigrants (and first generation residents) rarely use community support services because (1) it requires admission of a public problem, which is not generally acceptable; (2) it upsets family patterns of problem solutions; and (3) it means Latinos must deal with an uncertain and often hostile "Anglo" or "American" world. Those individuals who belong to church congregations may find support within the congregation or use the congregation and the priest/minister as a broker to "outside" services.

# 5.
# Language and Bilingualism

0421. Amastae, Jon and Elias-Olivares, Lucia, eds. Spanish in the United States: Sociolinguistic Aspects. New York: Cambridge University Press, 1982. 438 pp.

Eighteen essays dealing with various aspects of language structure and language uses by Chicanos, Puerto Ricans, and Cubans in the U.S. They approach the investigation from three viewpoints: (1) language variation and varieties of Spanish in the U.S.; (2) aspects of language contact and change; and (3) the ethnography of language uses in bilingual communities. Most of the essays are reprinted from earlier sources.

0422. Burke, Fred G. "Bilingualism/Biculturalism in American Education: An Adventure in Wonderland." Annals of the American Academy of Political and Social Science, Vol. 454 (March 1981), pp. 164-177.

0423. Edwards, J.R. "Current Issues in Bilingual Education." Ethnicity, Vol. 3, No. 1 (March 1976), pp. 70-81.

0424. Fishman, J. et al. Language Loyalty in the United States: The Maintenance and Perpetuation of Non-English Mother Tongues by American Ethnic and Religious Groups. Atlantic Highlands, NJ: Mouton-Humanities, 1966.

0425. John, Vera P. and Horner, Vivian M. Early Childhood Bilingual Education. New York: Modern Language Association, 1971.

0426. Kloss, Heinz. "Language Rights of Immigrant Groups." International Migration Review, Vol. 5, No. 2 (Summer 1971), pp. 250-267.

0427. LaFontaine, Herman et al., eds. Bilingual Education. Garden City Park, NY: Avery Publications, 1979.

0428. Padilla, R., ed. Ethnoperspectives in Bilingual Education Research: Bilingual Education and Public Policy in the United States. Ypsilanti, MI: Eastern Michigan University, 1979.

0429. Ridge, M., ed. The New Bilingualism: An American Dilemma. Los Angeles: Center for Study of American Experience, 1982. 272 pp.

This volume explores the issues inherent in bilingualism and biculturalism. Bilingualism as a means to the ideals of equal opportunity is examined.

0430. San Juan Cafferty, Pastora. "The Language Question: The Dilemma of Bilingual Education for Hispanics in America." In Ethnic Relations in America. Ed., Lance Liebman. Englewood Cliffs: Prentice-Hall, 1982, pp. 101-127.

This article addresses questions which must be answered in order to create a proper bilingual educational policy. The need for bilingual education for Hispanics is discussed in the context of the special dynamics of Hispanic immigration. Federal bilingual educational programs since 1968 are evaluated and their limitations pointed out.

# 6.
# Political Behavior and Organization

0431. Antunes, George and Gaitz, Charles M. "Ethnicity and Participation: A Study of Mexican-Americans, Blacks, and Whites." American Journal of Sociology, Vol. 80, No. 5 (March 1975), pp. 1192-1211.

> This study, based on survey data from Houston, Texas, partially supports the hypothesis that, because of a process of "compensation" or "ethnic identification," members of disadvantaged ethnic groups have higher levels of social and political participation than persons of the same social class who are members of the dominant group. When social class is controlled, Black levels of participation generally exceed or equal those of Whites; however, levels of participation among Mexican-Americans tend to be lower than those of Whites.

0432. Browning, Rufus P. "Blacks and Hispanics in California City Politics: Changes in Representation." Public Affairs Report, Vol. 20 (June 1979), pp. 1-9.

0433. Dreyfuss, Joel. "Blacks and Hispanics: Coalition or Confrontation?" Black Enterprise, Vol. 9 (July 1979), pp. 21-23.

0434. Elkin, Stephen L. "Political Structure, Political Organization, and Race." Politics and Society, Vol. 8, No. 2 (1978), pp. 225-251.

0435. Galvin, Miles and Gonzalez, Edward, Jr. "Reaching Out: New York's Hispanic Leadership Training Project." Labor Studies Journal, Vol. 7, No. 1 (Spring 1982), pp. 3-19.

0436. Henry, Keith S. "The Black Political Tradition in New York: A Conjunction of Political Cultures." Journal of Black Studies, Vol. 7 (June 1977), pp. 455-484.

0437. Infante, Isa Maria. "Politicalization of Immigrant Women From Puerto Rico and the Dominican Republic." Ph.D. dissertation, University of California, Riverside, 1977. 248 pp. (DAI: 36/06A, p. 3700)

> This study examines immigrant women living in New York and California in order to determine to what extent they become active participants in the

political process and whether this incorporation leads to feminism.  It shows that in order for Puerto Rican and Dominican immigrant women to have become feminists, they had to have undergone the following sequence:  (1) deviancy from the social norms in the islands; (2) resocialization through participation in organizational activity; (3) exposure to women's issues and activities in the U.S.; (4) independence from traditional social networks; and (5) exclusive participation in autonomous women's organizations.

0438.  Jamieson, Alfred.  Minorities and Politics.  Boston: Allyn and Bacon, 1977.  119 pp.

0439.  Miyares, Marcelino.  Models of Political Participation of Hispanic Americans.  New York: Arno Press, 1980.

0440.  Nelson, Dale C.  "Assimilation, Acculturation, and Political Participation."  Policy, Vol. 15, No. 1 (Fall 1982), pp. 26-47.

This survey study of a sample of American Black, Cuban, Dominican, Irish, Jewish, and Puerto Rican residents in New York City validates the standard assimilation model of ethnic politics.  It finds that ethnic group member-ship--regardless of assimilation, length of residence, educational level, or socioeconomic mobility--continues to make for substantial differences between ethnic groups with regard to political attitudes and participation.

0441.  Pavlak, Thomas J.  Ethnic Identification and Political Behavior.  San Francisco:  R and E Research Associates, 1976.  108 pp.

0442.  Salces, Luis M.  "Spanish Americans' Search for Political Representation: The 1975 Aldermanic Election in Chicago."  Journal of Political and Military Sociology, Vol. 6 (Fall 1978), pp. 175-187.

0443.  Tobias, H. J. and Woodhouse, C. E., eds.  Politics and Minorities.  Albuquerque, New Mexico:  University of New Mexico Press, 1969.

# 7.
# Literature of Immigrant Experience

0444. Baglin, Roger F. "The Mainland Experience in Selected Puerto Rican Literary Works." Ph.D. dissertation, State University of New York at Buffalo, 1971. (DAI: 32/06A, p. 3290)

0445. Coulthard, G.R. "The West Indian Novel of Immigration." Phylon, Vol. 20, No. 1 (Spring 1959), pp. 32-41.

> Analyzes the novels of immigration by four Caribbean writers: Guillermo Cotto-Thorner (Puerto Rican), Joseph Zobel (Martinican), Samuel Selvon (Trinidadian), and George Lamming (Barbadian).

0446. Guy, Rosa. Ruby. New York: Delco Press, 1976.

0447. Lacovia, R. M. "Migration and Transmutation in the Novels of McKay, Marshall, and Clarke." Journal of Black Studies, Vol. 7, No. 4 (June 1977), pp. 437-454.

> The portrait of the Caribbean emigrant to North America in the works of the three novelists is discussed. Characters from their novels are used to illustrate the theme of migration as a quest for transmutation. Focus is on the emigrant's change in sex role behavior and value orientation.

0448. Laviera, Tats. La Carreta Made a U-Turn. Gary: Arte Publico Press, 1979.

> Collection of poems by a Puerto Rican who grew up in the streets of New York. The poetry is bilingual both in style and in conception. These poems depict the conditions of New York's Puerto Ricans, and voice their defiance and pride. The overall thrust of the poems is a national affirmation and Afro-Caribbean orientation.

0449. McKay, Claude. Harlem Shadows. New York: Harcourt Brace, 1922.

0450. McKay, Claude. Home to Harlem. New York: Harper & Brothers, 1928.

0451. McKay, Claude. Banjo. New York: Harper & Brothers, 1929.

The story of a group of Black emigrants—from Africa, the Caribbean, and the United States—living in Marseille, France, during the 1920s.

0452. McKay, Claude. A Long Way from Home. New York: Furman, 1936.

0453. Marshall, Paule. Brown Girl, Brownstones. New York: Random House, 1959.

0454. Marshall, Paule. Soul Clap Hands and Sing. New York: Atheneum, 1961.

0455. Marshall, Paule. The Chosen Place, the Timeless People. New York: Harcourt, Brace and World, 1969.

0456. Marshall, Paule. "Black Immigrant Women in Brown Girl, Brownstones." In Female Immigrants to the United States. Eds., D. M. Mortimer and R. S. Bryce-Laporte. Washington, DC: Smithsonian Institution, Research Institute on Immigration and Ethnic Studies, Occasional Papers No. 2, 1981, pp, 3-13.

The novelist reminisces on the lives of Barbadian immigrant women during the years following World War I. She juxtaposes these real life immigrants with the women characters in her novel.

0457. Mohr, Eugene V. The Nuyorican Experience:  Literature of the Puerto Rican Minority. Westport, CT: Greenwood Press, 1983. 160 pp.

0458. Murray, Pauli. Proud Shoes:  The Story of an American Family. New York: Harper-Row, 1965.

0459. Pietri, Pedro. Puerto Rican Obituary. New York: Monthly Review Press, 1973.

0460. Rivera, Edward. Family Installments:  Memories of Growing Up Hispanic. New York: William Morrow, 1982.

A family chronicle bordering between autobiography and fiction. The author is a Puerto Rican who grew up in New York's El Barrio. The chronicle begins with a fictional reconstruction of the family's history in Puerto Rico. It is followed by the story of the family's migration to New York and its life there. This part contains many comic episodes of the immigrants' adjustment.

0461. Soto, Pedro Juan. Spiks. New York: Monthly Review Press, 1973.

A collection of short stories about Puerto Ricans in New York and San Juan. Most of the characters are women "fighting to break out of the suffocating prisons of family and society in which they are held."

0462. Soto, Pedro Juan. Hot Land, Cold Season. New York: Dell, 1973.

A young Puerto Rican raised in New York returned to the island. He found himself trapped in limbo where he was neither American nor Puerto Rican. This is the story of his unsuccessful struggle to overcome his identity crisis.

0463. Thomas, Piri. Down These Mean Streets. New York: The New American Library, 1967.

0464. Thomas, Piri. Savior, Savior, Hold My Hand. New York: Doubleday, 1972.

0465.  Thomas, Piri. Seven Long Times. New York: Praeger, 1974.

The above three novels make up a connected, somewhat chronologically overlapping triology.  Together they are a semi-autobiographical narrative of the Puerto Rican author's life.  The story traces a Puerto Rican's journey through the life-cycle and his many dramatic experiences:  growing up, schooling, street gangs, imprisonment, religious conversion, and relationships with other ethnic groups.

0466.  Thomas, Piri. Stories From El Barrio. New York: Knopf, 1978.

0467.  White, Edgar. Sati: The Rastifarian. New York: Lothrop, Lee and Shepard, 1973.

# V. Studies of Black Immigrant Groups

# 1.
# Africans in the United States

0468. "African Students in America." Sepia, Vol. 10 (1961), pp. 32-34.

0469. Becker, Tamar. "Black Africans and Black Americans on an American Campus: The African View." Sociology and Social Research, Vol. 57, No. 2 (January 1973), pp. 168-181.

> This article explores the manifestations and causes of strained relations between Africans and Black Americans on the UCLA campus. Higher status and tangible benefits accorded Africans in preference to Black Americans, sociocultural differences between the groups, and perceived rejection by Blacks strengthen the Africans' inclination to emphasize their separate identity and to minimize contact with Black Americans.

0470. Bryan, Dorothy Payne. "Nigerian Women and Child-Rearing Practices in Washington, DC: A Summary of Research Findings and Implications." In Female Immigrants to the United States. Eds., D. M. Mortimer and R. S. Bryce-Laporte. Washington, DC: Smithsonian Institution, Research Institute on Immigration and Ethnic Studies, Occasional Papers No. 2, 1981, pp. 157-170.

0471. Chukunta, N. K. Onusha, ed. "A Special Issue on Brain Drain from Africa." Issue, Vol. 9, No. 4 (Winter 1979).

0472. Clausen, Edwin and Bermingham, Jack. Chinese and African Professionals in California: A Case Study of Equality and Opportunity in the United States. Washington, DC: University Press of America, 1982. 134 pp.

> This monography investigates the role of racism in the lives of the two immigrant groups. It also addresses the question of public policy and its role in the implementation of measures to correct the class and institutional oppression faced by these immigrants.

0473. Da Silva, Paulo Vierira. "African and Latin American Graduate Students' Assessment of Situations Related to Their Academic Life in the United States." Ph.D. dissertation, University of Southern California, 1974. 282 pp. (DAI: 35/02A, p. 834)

A questionnaire was administered to 126 African and Latin American graduate students at the University of Southern California in 1973, and the data validate the hypothesis that the two groups had essentially the same perceptions about specific situations related to their personal, social, and academic experiences.

0474.  Davis, J.; Hanson, R. and Burnor, D.  The African Students:  His Achievements and His Problems.  New York: Institute of International Education, 1961.

0475.  Fafunwa, B.  "An African Student Looks at America."  Negro Digest, Vol. 11 (1961), pp. 41-44.

0476.  Isaacs, Harold R.  "The American Negro and Africa:  Some Notes."  Phylon, Vol. 20, No. 3 (Fall 1959), pp. 219-233.

The image of Africa has rarely been examined in studies of Afro-American personality and life.  Through interviews the author finds that the negative image of Africa in the U.S. influences childhood learning and leads Afro-Americans to dissociate themselves from their African origins.

0477.  Moikobu, Josephine Moraa.  "The Relationships Between Black-Americans and African Students:  An Exploratory Study."  Ph.D. dissertation, State University of New York at Binghamton, 1978. 253 pp.  (DAI: 39/05A, p. 3154)

This study of 40 Black American and 40 African students in Buffalo, New York, examines what the two groups feel they have in common with one another.  More Africans feel that they have internal dimensions of identity (color/ancestry) with Black Americans, whereas more Black Americans choose external dimensions of identity (political, social, and economic oppression/suppression) as what they feel they have in common with Africans.

0478.  Morgan, Gordon D.  "Exploratory Study of Problems of Academic Adjustment of Nigerian Students in America."  Journal of Negro Education, Vol. 32, No. 3 (Summer 1963), pp. 208-217.

This study compares Nigerian and other foreign students in terms of adjustment problems and analyzes these problems in a value context.  In relation to prior academic preparation, instructor demands, and language difficulty, Nigerian students did not perceive their problems as being appreciably different from those of selected other minority groups.  However, they believed their problems were greater than those of the White majority.

0479.  Nagenda, John.  "Pride or Prejudice?  Relationships Between Africans and American Negroes."  Race, Vol. 9, No. 2 (October 1967), 159-171.

Describes the author's (a Ugandan) encounters with Black Americans.  He found that Africans have made less attempt to identify with American Blacks than vice versa.  This is due to the fact that Africans have better opportunity to enjoy dignity in their own lands than American Blacks in theirs.

0480.  Odenyo, Amos O.  "Africans and Afro-Americans on Campus:  A Study of Some of the Relationships Between Two Minority Sub-Communities."  Ph.D. dissertation, University of Minnesota, 1970. 265 pp.  (DAI: 32/01A, p. 555)

Examines the quasi-community formation of African and Afro-American
students on campus, and examines the possible ambivalent attitudes of the
two groups. The study finds that the ambivalence of Africans toward Afro-
Americans rests on (1) the fear of identification with an underprivileged
minority; (2) what the former perceive as the exaggeration or distortion of
African culture by the latter. Conversely, the ambivalence of Afro-Americans
toward Africans is due to (1) the former's perception of the latter as free,
high-status foreigners without the stigma of slavery; (2) the Africans' nega-
tion of Afro-Americans' perception of Africa and its culture; (3) Afro-
Americans' perception of American society as technologically superior; (4)
the apparent failure of Africans to endorse the assumption advanced by
Afro-Americans that Black people all over the world should join together in
an effort at liberation. Finally, the mutual ambivalence between the two
groups is reinforced by the fact that they view each other as foreign despite
the commonality of ancestral homeland.

0481. "Refugees from the African Continent." Encore, Vol. 4 (November 24,
1975), pp. 20-21.

0482. Roberts, N. "What Nigerian Students Think of Us." Sepia, Vol. 9 (March
1961), pp. 18-20

0483. Rustin, Bayard. "How Black Americans See Black Africans - and Vice
Versa." In Down the Line. Chicago: Quadrangle Books, 1971, pp. 255-258.

The relationship between Africans and Afro-Americans is one of ambivalence.
There is a major difference between the two groups in that the former are
a majority in their societies, while the latter are a minority. The struggle
for self-rule and independence by the former should not be imitated by the
latter. It is only when Black Americans have lost hope in America and lost
their identity as Americans that they seek to establish their identity as
Africans.

0484. Skinner, Elliott P. "African, Afro-American, White American: A Case of
Pride and Prejudice." Freedomways, Vol. 5 (Summer 1965), pp. 380-395.

0485. Veroff, Joseph. "African Students in the United States." Journal of Social
Issues, Vol. 19, No. 3 (July 1963), 48-60.

This study based on questionaire survey and interviews finds that African
students in the U.S. tend to become more tolerant of the American's infor-
mality and more sensitive to any insincere outgoingness Americans exhibit.
They seem to become more interested in nationalistic ideas and less involved
in Pan-Africanist identifications. They tend to have higher achievement
risk preference the longer they have been in the U.S.

0486. Weisbord, R. "Africa, Africans, and the Afro-American: Images and Identities in Transition." Race, Vol. 10, No. 3 (January 1969), 305-321.

Traces the historical development of Black nationalism, Pan-Africanism,
and back-to-Africa movement. Points out that the quest of Afro-Americans
is basically for identity as well as power. The author concludes that historically when conditions for American Blacks worsened, consciousness of
Africa was heightened. In recent years, there has been an increasing identification with Africa among those American Blacks who nevertheless were
fully committed to integration into the American social fabric.

# 2.
# Caribbeans in the
# United States: General

0487. Bryce-Laporte, Roy S. "Black Immigrants: The Experience of Invisibility and Inequality." Journal of Black Studies, Vol. 3, No. 1 (September 1972), pp. 29-56.

Black immigrants are perhaps the least visible of American ethnic constituencies: much of their presence, their contributions, and their problems go unattended in the larger society. In fact, they suffer double invisibility on the national level —as Blacks and as Black foreigners. The Black immigrants are pushed more by the adverse socioeconomic conditions of their country than by its subtle racism, and they are pulled by the relatively open socioeconomic opportunity structure of the U.S. more than they are repelled by its rigid and institutionalized racial practices. The average Black immigrant is usually highly disposed to be an ardent practioner of the Protestant Ethic and true tester of the American Dream.

0488. Bryce-Laporte, Roy S. "Black Immigrants." In Through Different Eyes: Black and White Perspectives on American Race Relations. Eds., Peter Rose, Stanley Rothman, and William J. Wilson. New York: Oxford University Press, 1973, pp. 44-71.

This is a slightly revised version of the author's "Black Immigrants: The Experience of Invisibility and Inequality."

0489. Bryce-Laporte, Roy S. "The United States' Role in Caribbean Migration: Background to the Problem." In Caribbean Migration to the United States. Eds., R. S. Bryce-Laporte and D. M. Mortimer. Washington, DC: Smithsonian Institution, Research Institute on Immigration and Ethnic Studies, Occasional Papers No. 1, 1976, pp. 1-14.

0490. Bryce-Laporte, Roy S. "Caribbean Migration to the United States: Some Tentative Conclusions." In Caribbean Migration to the United States. Eds., R. S. Bryce-Laporte and D. M. Mortimer. Washington, DC: Smithsonian Institution, Research Institute on Immigration and Ethnic Studies, Occasional Papers No. 1, 1976, pp. 193-204.

0491. Bryce-Laporte, Roy Simon. "New York City and the New Caribbean Immigration: A Contextual Statement." International Migration Review, Vol. 13, No. 2 (Summer 1979), pp. 214-234.

Discusses the socio-historical, demographic and cultural aspects of Caribbean migration to New York. The Caribbean emigration movement is an old one and predominantly urban in character. The recent increase in the Caribbean presence in New York City brings changes in its cultural and ethnic configuration, greater cosmopolitization, and international linkages.

0492. Bryce-Laporte, Roy Simon and Mortimer, Delores M., eds. Caribbean Migration to the United States. Washington, DC: Smithsonian Institution, Research Institute on Immigration and Ethnic Studies, Occasional Papers No. 1, 1976.

0493. Bryce-Laporte, Roy S. and Couch, S.R. Exploratory Fieldwork on Latino Migrants and Indochinese Refugees. Washington, DC: Smithsonian Institution, Research Institute on Immigration and Ethnic Studies, Research Notes No. 1, 1976. 139 pp.

0494. Center for Latin American Studies. Caribbean Migration Program. University of Florida, Gainesville, 1982. 33 pp.

0495. Dominguez, Virginia R. "The Spanish-Speaking Caribbeans in New York: The Middle Race." Revista Interamericana/Interamerican Review, Vol. 3, No. 2 (1973), pp. 135-142.

Discusses the issues of social interaction and ethnic identity among adolescents of Cuban, Puerto Rican, and Dominican extraction in Washington Heights. The main concern is the differential perception and social manipulation of physical appearance between Caribbean populations and American society, or the consequences of self-identification of the "Middle Race." The major problem of social interaction in this community is the constant reaffirmation of internal social ordering vis-a-vis the social equalization imposed from the outside.

0496. Dominguez, Virginia R. From Neighbor to Stranger: The Dilemma of Caribbean Peoples in the United States. New Haven: Yale University Antilles Research Program, Occasional Papers No. 5, 1975. 177 pp.

A comparative study of various groups of Caribbean immigrants in terms of their differential patterns of adaptation, social mobility, and residential dispersion. Caribbean populations are grouped into three categories: the immigrants (British West Indians, Haitians, Dominicans); the refugees (Cubans); and the citizens (Puerto Ricans). The author argues that Caribbean populations should be treated as an analytical unit because of their common colonial background and their mental and physical similarities as seen by Americans at large. On the other hand, there are enough differences among Caribbean populations that they should be treated as separate units. The particularity of each group rests on the characteristics of the home country and the tie between migrants and islanders. Finally, the author suggests that, in light of current pluralistic ideology and the rise of ethnic consciousness, assimilation will never really succeed with large sectors of Caribbean populations in the United States. The book includes numerous statistical tables and an extensive bibliography.

0497. Dominguez, Virginia. "Show Your Colors: Ethnic Divisiveness Among Hispanic Caribbean Migrants." Migration Today, Vol. 6 (February 1978), pp. 5-9.

0498. Fitzpatrick, J.P. and Gurak, D.T. Hispanic Intermarriage in New York City: 1975. Bronx, NY: Hispanic Research Center, Fordham University, 1979. 100 pp.

0499. Gordon, Monica H. "In Search of the Means to a Better Life: Caribbean Migration to the United States." Contributions in Black Studies, No. 5 (1981-82), pp. 28-42.

   Discusses the social, economic, and political problems of the Caribbean area which have resulted in the continous flows of emigration. Also briefly discusses the consequences of migration to the sending and receiving societies.

0500. Lamur, Humphrey E. and Speckmann, John D., eds. Adaptation of Migrants From the Caribbean in the European and American Metropolis. Symposium of the 34th Annual Conference of American Society for Applied Anthropology. Amsterdam, 1978. 201 pp.

0501. Lowenthal, David. "West Indian Emigrants Overseas." In Caribbean Social Relations. Ed., Colin G. Clarke. Liverpool: Center for Latin American Studies, University of Liverpool, 1978, pp. 82-94.

   A general account of similarities and differences between the experiences and adjustment of Caribbean immigrants in Britain, France, the Netherlands, and the United States.

0502. McCoy, Terry L. and Wood, Charles H. Caribbean Workers in the Florida Sugar Cane Industry. Gainesville: Center for Latin American Studies, University of Florida, Occasional Papers No. 2, 1982. 75 pp.

0503. Mortimer, Delores M. "Caribbean Immigrants: Some Further Perspectives on Their Lives." In Caribbean Migration to the United States. Eds., R. S. Bryce-Laporte and D. M. Mortimer. Washington, DC: Smithsonian Institution, Research Institute on Immigration and Ethnic Studies, Occasional Papers No. 1, 1976, pp. 182-192.

   An account on the effect of immigration on professionals from the Caribbean, including international employees, diplomats, and students.

0504. Palmer, R. W. "Migration from the Caribbean to the United States: The Economic Status of the Immigrants." In Caribbean Migration to the United States. Eds., R. S. Bryce-Laporte and D. M. Mortimer. Washington, DC: Smithsonian Institution, Research Institute on Immigration and Ethnic Studies, Occasional Papers No. 1, 1976, pp. 44-54.

0505. Senior, Clarence O. Our Citizens from the Caribbean. New York: McGraw-Hill, 1965.

0506. Stinner, William F. and de Albuquerque, Klaus. "The Dynamics of Caribbean Return Migration." In Return Migration and Remittances: Developing a Caribbean Perspective. Eds., William F. Stinner, Klaus de Albuquerque and Roy S. Bryce-Laporte. Washington, DC: Smithsonian Institution, Research Institute on Immigration and Ethnic Studies, Occasional Papers No. 3, 1982, pp. xxxvii-1xvii.

An overview of the subject. The authors present a framework for studying Caribbean return migration, which includes three major dimensions: (1) attributes of the return flow, including its prevalence, selectivity, and direction; (2) the motivations for return and their relations to structural and individual conditions; and (3) the consequences of return migration for the returnees as well as the original sending society.

0507.  Stinner, William F.; de Albuquerque, Klaus and Bryce-Laporte, Roy S., eds.  Return Migration and Remittances:  Developing a Caribbean Perspective. Washington, DC: Smithsonian Institution, Research Institute on Immigration and Ethnic Studies, Occasional Papers No. 3, 1982.  322 pp.

This volume is divided into two parts:  Part I includes eight papers on return migrations to various Caribbean countries; Part II contains three papers on remittances.  Each part also includes an extensive bibliography.  Some articles are separately annotated in this Bibliography.

0508.  Sutton, Constance.  "Caribbean Migrants and Group Identity: Suggestions for Comparation Analysis."  In Migration: Report on the Research Conference on Migration, Ethnic Minority Status and Social Adaptation.  Eds., Otto Klineberg and George DeVos.  Rome:  U.N. Social Defense Research Institute, 1973.

# 3.
# West Indians in the United States

0509. Anderson, Jervis "Uprootedness." Commentary, Vol. 40, No. 2 (August 1965), pp. 63-67.

The author, a journalist and writer, reminisces on his growing up in Jamaica and his impressions and reactions when he first arrived in the United States.

0510. Anthony-Welch, Lillian D. "A Comparative Analysis of the Black Woman As Transmitter of Black Values, Based on Case Studies of Families in Ghana and Among Jamaicans and Afro-Americans in Hartford, Connecticut." Ed.D. dissertation, University of Massachusetts, 1976. 413 pp. (DAI: 37/11A, p. 6895)

This study is based on three case studies of a mother and her family in each of the three ethnic groups. The author identifies and defines 23 Black cultural values, and arrives at three major conclusions: (1) viable cultural values exist among the three groups; (2) these values have an African origin; and (3) the Black woman is a prime transmitter of viable cultural values.

0511. Best, Tony. "West Indians and Afro-Americans: A Partnership." The Crisis, Vol. 82 (December 1975), pp. 389-393.

0512. Blackett, Richard. "Some of the Problems Confronting West Indians in the Black American Struggle." Black Lines, Vol. 1, No. 4 (1971).

0513. Bolles, A. Lynn. "'Goin' Abroad': Working Class Jamaican Women and Migration." In Female Immigrants to the United States. Eds., D. M. Mortimer and R. S. Bryce-Laporte. Washington, DC: Smithsonian Institution, Research Institute on Immigration and Ethnic Studies, Occasional Papers No. 2, 1981, pp. 56-84.

Discusses the economic conditions of Jamaica which foster emigration and the characteristics of prospective emigrants among working-class women.

0514. Bonnett, Aubrey W. "Instrumental and Expressive Voluntary Organizations Among Black West Indian Immigrants in New York." Journal of Voluntary Action Research, Vol. 6 (1977), pp. 89-97.

0515. Bonnett, Aubrey W. Institutional Adaptation of West Indian Immigrants to America: An Analysis of Rotating Credit Associations. Washington, DC: University Press of America, 1981. 142 pp.

This sociological study provides a comparison of the practice and function of rotating credit associations in both developing and developed countries. The case of the West Indian immigrants in Brooklyn, New York, is then analyzed in detail. Two major findings are presented: (1) the credit associations are a generational adaptive mechanism for the first-generation immigrants, but they do not function as a symbol of ethnic identity; (2) their pattern of use is strongly influenced by parental use.

0516. Bonnett, Aubrey W. "Structured Adaptation of Black Migrants from the Caribbean: An Examination of an Indigenous Banking System in Brooklyn." Phylon, Vol. 42, No. 4 (December 1981), pp. 346-355.

This paper analyzes the institution of rotating credit associations as found in the West Indies and transplanted to Brooklyn by immigrants. The institution serves less as a symbol of ethnic pride than as an economically adaptive mechanism for the immigrants, especially in meeting their financial needs.

0517. Bourne-Vanneck, Richard P. "Toward Another World: A West Indian at Yale." Crisis, Vol. 81 (February 1974), pp. 43-46.

0518. Buckley, Tom. "Calypso Finds Brooklyn a Home Away from Home." New York Times (June 12, 1974), p. 47.

0519. Burgess, Judith and James-Gray, Meryl. "Migration and Sex Roles: A Comparison of Black and Indian Trinidadians in New York City." In Female Immigrants to the United States. Eds., D. M. Mortimer and R. S. Bryce-Laporte. Washington, DC: Smithsonian Institution, Research Institute on Immigration and Ethnic Studies, Occasional Papers No. 2, 1981, pp. 85-111.

This study is based on interviews with 28 Trinidadians in New York City. Comparisons are made between Black and Indian Trinidadians with respect to three variables as they are affected by immigration experience: (1) social mobility and economic attainment; (2) racial minority identification; and (3) changes in sex roles and family relationships.

0520. Carnegie, Charles V. "Strategic Flexibility in the West Indies: A Social Psychology of Caribbean Migration." Caribbean Review, Vol. 11, No. 1 (Winter 1982), pp. 10-13, 54.

Strategic flexibility is an important trait of the cultural and psychological make-up of Caribbean peoples. It is manifest in the ability to adjust rapidly to whatever comes along and the actual building of multiple options. It can thus be argued that Caribbean migrants may not see themselves as such. The Caribbean migrants, in crossing the boundaries of the nation-state, are not acting out an aberration but are doing something for which their culture has prepared them.

0521. Clarke, J. H. "West Indian Partisans in the Fight for Freedom." Negro Digest, Vol. 15 (July 1966), pp. 18-25.

0522. Coombs, Orde. "Illegal Immigrants in New York: The Invisible Subculture." New York, Vol. 9, No. 11 (March 15, 1976), pp. 33-41.

Describes the life of an illegal West Indian immigrant in New York City. The author contends that because of their illegal status these immigrants have been forced to adopt a mantle of conspiracy and deceit. They learn that to lie is to survive in this country, that laws are made to be broken, and that deviousness is the passport to success.

0523. Coombs, Orde. "West Indians in New York: Moving Beyond the Limbo Pole." New York, Vol. 3, No. 28 (July 13, 1970), pp. 28-32.

The author, an immigrant from St. Vincent, describes West Indians' strong commitment to middle-class values, their "integrationist fantasies," and their claim to superiority to native Blacks. These illusions are challenged by the militant Black Power movement both in the U.S. and in the islands.

0524. de Albuquerque, Klaus and McElroy, Jerome L. "West Indian Migration to the United States Virgin Islands: Demographic Impacts and Socioeconomic Consequences." International Migration Review, Vol. 16, No. 1 (Spring, 1982), pp. 61-101.

This article examines the movement of West Indians to the USVI in recent decades. The principal emphasis concerns the impacts of this heavy immigration on these demographic features: population size, population distribution, population density, age and sex composition, natality, fertility and marriage, mortality, and ethnic composition. The article also briefly discusses the socioeconomic inequities suffered by the West Indians: insecure legal status, persistent job and wage discrimination, grudging social acceptance and political disenfranchisement.

0525. DeWind, Josh et al. "Caribbean Migration: Contract Labor in U.S. Agriculture." NACLA Report on the Americas, Vol. 11, No. 8 (November/December 1977), pp. 4-37.

Examines the working conditions of West Indian contract workers employed in the U.S. agriculture. A detailed case study is made of the West Indian cane cutters in Florida. A comparison is made between this H-2 contract labor program and a similar contract system established by the Puerto Rican Government. The article highlights the helplessness of contract laborers and the undermining role the contract programs play in the attempts of workers to improve their conditions of work.

0526. Ebanks, G.; George, P.M. and Nobbe, C.E. "Emigration from Barbados, 1951-1970." Social and Economic Studies, Vol. 28, No. 2 (June 1979), pp. 431-449.

An analysis of emigration from Barbados to the Great Britain, Canada, and the U.S., based on interviews, statistics, and secondary sources.

0527. Foner, Nancy. "West Indians in New York City and London: A Comparative Analysis." International Migration Review, Vol. 13, No. 2 (Summer 1979), pp. 284-297.

West Indians in the United States are occupationally more successful than West Indians in Britain. The author proposes three factors to explain this difference. (1) A higher percentage of West Indians in the U.S. have lived there longer than is the case in Britain. (2) West Indian migration to the U.S. in the past two decades has been marked by a higher percentage of

professionals and other non-manual workers than the earlier emigration to
Britain. (3) West Indians in the U.S. have the advantage of being a part of a
large native Black population.

0528. Foner, Nancy and Napoli, Richard. "Jamaican and Black-American Migrant
Farm Workers: A Comparative Analysis." Social Problems, VoL 25, No. 5 (June
1978), pp. 491-503.

In contrast to Black-American migrant farm workers in the Northeast region,
this study of Jamaican migrant farm workers in a New York camp shows
that they are very productive and save most of their earnings. This is explained
by two factors: (1) the relative value of the wages paid to Jamaicans and
Black Americans and (2) the actual, as well as perceived, opportunities for
mobility of each group of migrants and their children.

0529. Forsythe, Dennis. "West Indian Radicalisms in America: An Assessment
of Ideology." In Ethnicity in Americas. Ed., Frances Henry. The Hague: Mouton,
1976, pp. 301-332.

The author sees West Indian radicalism in North America as a response of an
ethnic and migrant group to a new social situation. The author suggests that
the radical propensity of West Indians in America is due to (1) the problem
and processes of migration which they encounter and go through as migrants
and which partly ensue from their expectations as migrants; (2) certain structural conditions in America which make protests possible. Four radical West
Indian ideologies are discussed: civic radicalism (W. A. Domingo); interna-
tionalist radicalism (C. L. R. James); Black radicalism (Marcus Garvey);
progressive radicalism (Claude McKay). These four ideologies are differentiated on the basis of their respective acceptance or rejection of capitalism,
white ethnocentrism, and white power.

0530. Forsythe, Dennis. "Black Immigrant and the American Ethos: Theories
and Observations." In Caribbean Migration to the United States. Eds., R. S.
Bryce-Laporte and D. M. Mortimer. Washington, DC: Smithsonian Institution,
Research Institute on Immigration and Ethnic Studies, Occasional Papers No. 1,
1976, pp. 55-82.

0531. Fraser, C. Gerald. "Neighborhoods: West Indies Flavor Bedford-Stuyvesant."
The New York Times (October 28, 1970).

0532. Fraser, C. Gerald. "The 'Union' Immigrants Built." Black Enterprise, VoL
10, No. 9 (April 1980), p. 31.

Describes the Paragon Progressive Credit Union, founded in 1941 by West
Indian Immigrants in Brooklyn and still functioning today.

0533. Girling, R. K. "The Migration of Human Capital from the Third World:
The Implications and Some Data from the Jamaican Case." Social and Economic
Studies, VoL 23, No. 1 (March 1974), pp. 84-96.

This article presents a human capital theory for the study of emigration. It
is argued that emigration of individuals with extensive social investment has
been an enormous welfare loss for Third World nations. The theory is then
illustrated by the Jamaican case with quantitative measures of the economic
impact of high skilled emigration.

0534. Glantz, Oscar. "Native Sons and Immigrants: Some Beliefs and Values of American-Born and West Indian Blacks at Brooklyn College." Ethnicity, Vol. 5, No. 2 (June 1978), pp. 189-202.

This study suggests that West Indian immigrants in Brooklyn, by contrast to their native-born counterparts, are marked by a high level of ambition, a passion for hard work, and a strong trust in the reward system. In these terms, they can be characterized as a vital and dynamic ethnic group, not only within the Black community but in the larger society as well.

0535. Glantzman, Abraham. "The Double Burden." New York West Indian (December 1968).

0536. Goddard, Lawford L. "Social Structure and Migration: A Comparative Study of the West Indies." Ph.D. dissertation, Stanford University, 1976. 322 pp. (DAI: 37/10A, p. 6784)

The author contends that structural factors, not individual values and decision, play the most important role in determining migration. The cases of Barbados, Jamaica, and Trinidad are used to test the model. The data suggest that post -WW II economic development in these countries created structural dependence on external capital and technology. The resultant high levels of unemployment, inadequate educational system, and failure in economic integration have contributed to the increase in emigration over time.

0537. Golden, Herbert M. "Five-Hundred and Seventy-Five West Indian, Southern and Northern American Born Black Elderly Living in the Poverty Areas of New York City: A Descriptive Analysis." Ed.D. dissertation, Columbia University Teachers College, 1977. 314 pp. (DAI: 380/01A, p. 511)

This descriptive-comparative study examines the factor of place of birth in the process of minority groups' adaptation to aging. Findings demonstrate that place of birth provides a functional approach toward gaining greater insight into the life styles and coping patterns of Black elderly living in the inner city of New York.

0538. Gonzalez, Nancie S. "Garifuna Settlement in New York: A New Frontier." International Migration Review, Vol. 13, No. 2 (Summer 1979), pp. 255-263.

The Garifuna (Black Caribs of Central America) have a long history of temporary and circular migration so the migration process is less disruptive to their home communities than might otherwise be the case. Garifuna immigrants in New York have retained their ethnic identity regardless of their association with the West Indian (English-speaking) and Caribbean (Spanish-speaking) peoples of that city.

0539. Gordon, Monica H. "Identification and Adaptation: A Study of Two Groups of Jamaican Immigrants in New York City." Ph.D. dissertation, City University of New York, 1979. 267 pp. (DAI: 39/12A, p. 7529)

This study compares the adaptation and identification patterns of immigrants who arrived in the U.S. (1) between 1920 and 1940 and (2) between 1960 and 1975. The early immigrants identified more strongly with America while the recent immigrants identified strongly with Jamaica. In terms of adaptation, the early group showed a pattern of cultural assimilation, while the recent group developed a pluralistic adaptation with a strong orientation toward Jamaican culture.

0540.  Gordon, Monica H.  "Caribbean Migration: A Perspective on Women." In Female Immigrants to the United States. Eds., D. M. Mortimer and R. S. Bryce-Laporte.  Washington, DC: Smithsonian Institution, Research Institute on Immigration and Ethnic Studies, Occasional papers No. 2, 1981, pp. 14-55.

This paper examines the social and economic conditions of women in the English-speaking Caribbean. Argues that women migrate in search of opportunities to meet family obligations and for self-improvement. Discusses the adjustment process of the women immigrants, focusing on family relations, education, occupation, income, and their assessment of their situation in the U.S.

0541.  Green, James W.  "The British West Indian Alien Labor Problem in the Virgin Islands." Caribbean Studies, Vol. 12, No. 4 (January 1973), pp. 56-75.

This article presents the historical background to West Indian immigration to the USVI. It discusses in detail the complex "job bonding" system under which immigrants are employed. The living conditions of the immigrants and the prejudice and discrimination they encounter in the host society are described.

0542.  Grove, Gene.  "American Scene: The West Indians." Tuesday, Vol. 2, No. 3 (1966), pp. 12-15.

0543.  Hellwig, David J.  "Black Meets Black: Afro-American Reactions to West Indian Immigrants in the 1920's." South Atlantic Quarterly, Vol. 77, (Spring 1978), pp. 206-224.

0544.  Henry, Keith S.  "The Place of the Culture of Migrant Commonwealth Afro-West Indians in the Political Life of Black New York in the Period Circa 1918 to Circa 1966." Ph.D. dissertation, University of Toronto, 1973. (DAI: 35/09A, p. 6208)

This study supports the view that West Indians played a disproportionately large role in both radical and conventional politics in New York. Argues that West Indian-American behavior was consistent with formative and specific influences of Caribbean culture, and with the experience of alien migration. Also points out that there were effective mutual influences between the native and immigrant Blacks in New York.

0545.  Henry, Keith S.  "The Black Political Tradition in New York: A Conjunction of Political Cultures." Journal of Black Studies, Vol. 7, No. 4 (June 1977), pp. 455-484.

This article explores three areas of the constantly evolving New York Black political tradition of the 20th century. The contributions of West Indian immigrants and native-born Blacks are compared. Street journalism and attention to international politics were major West Indian contributions, while female participation in conventional politics and public affairs was a native development. The article then gives a brief account of the growth of a political sense of community in Black New York.

0546. Hope, Kempe R. "The Emigration of High-level Manpower from Developing to Developed Countries (with Reference to Trinidad and Tobago)." International Migration, Vol. 14, No. 3 (1976), pp. 209-218.

0547. Hoyt, V. "The Occupational and Social Adjustment of the British West Indian Immigrant in Manhattan." M.A. thesis, New York University, 1941.

0548. James, S. M. "When Your Patient Is Black West Indian." American Journal of Nursing, Vol. 78 (November 1978), pp. 1908-1909.

0549. Johnson, Audrey. "Ethnic, Racial Attitudes Among Professional and Managerial Black Women: Research Note." In Female Immigrants to the United States. Eds., D. M. Mortimer and R. S. Bryce-Laporte. Washington, DC: Smithsonian Institution, Research Institute on Immigration and Ethnic Studies, Occasional Paper No. 2, 1981, pp. 143-156.

   A comparison of American Blacks and West Indian immigrants regarding their perceptions of (1) educational opportunities; (2) family life style; (3) racial and class discrimination. Data indicate there are salient differences, and that intraracial assimilation has not yet taken place.

0550. Justus, Joyce Bennett. "Strategies for Survival: West Indians in Los Angeles." In Adaptation of Migrants from the Caribbean in the European and American Metropolis. Eds., H. E. Lamur and J. D. Speckmann. Symposium of the 34th Annual Conference of the American Society for Applied Anthropology, 1978, pp. 112-129.

   Lower-class West Indians perceive migration as a temporary phase, whereas high status immigrants see it as something more permanent. The middle class incorporates elements of both orientations. Those who say that their stay in the U.S. is temporary are likely to choose a club with exclusive West Indian membership as the focus of social interaction. If the migrant does not intend to return to the West Indies, his/her choice of strategy is guided by a desire both to maintain his/her position as a stranger and to engage in social interaction with the larger society.

0551. Justus, Joyce B. "West Indians in Los Angeles: Community and Identity." In Caribbean Migration to the United States. Eds., R. S. Bryce-Laporte and D. M. Mortimer. Washington, DC: Smithsonian Institution, Research Institute on Immigration and Ethnic Studies, Occasional Papers No. 1, 1976, pp. 130-148.

0552. Koslofsky, Joanne. "'Going Foreign' - Causes of Jamaican Migration." NACLA Report on the Americas, Vol. 15, No. 1 (January/February 1981), pp. 2-31.

   The pattern of migration from the underdeveloped to the advanced capitalist countries is determined by a mode of international development predicated on capital's unceasing drive for profit. This is illustrated in this case study by the process in which agribusiness expansion led to massive emigration of Jamaica's rural population. The domination of transnational sugar corporations, which aggravated the problems of unemployment and poverty, is the fundamental cause of Jamaican emigration.

0553. Marshall, Dawn I. "The History of Caribbean Migrations: The Case of the West Indies." Caribbean Review, Vol. 11, No. 1 (Winter 1982), pp. 6-9, 52-53.

The history of migration in the Commonwealth Caribbean since Emancipation is divided into four phases: (1) 1835-1885, dominated by inter-territorial movement; (2) 1885-1920, dominated by the movement to Panama; (3) 1920-1940, there was little out-migration although there was some forced repatriation and voluntary return migration; (4) since 1940, dominated by movement to the metropolitan countries of the United Kingdom and North America. The need to emigrate, especially to the U.S., is not likely to diminish in the near future.

0554.  Maynard, Edward S. "Endogamy Among Barbadian Immigrants to New York City: An Exploratory Study of Marriage Patterns and Their Relationship to Adjustment to an Alien Culture." Ph.D. dissertation, New York University, 1972. 140 pp. (DAI: 37/11B, p. 5107)

This is an anthropological investigation of the function of endogamy as an adjustment mechanism among Barbadian immigrants. Four major conclusions are presented: (1) there is a high probability for Barbadian immigrants to marry endogamously and refuse American Blacks as marriage partners, as they perceive the latter to be in an inferior social position; (2) there is no significant relationship between time interval and endogamous marriage; (3) there is a positive relationship between church attendance and endogamous marriage, as the church serves as a screening device and aids in the persistence of endogamy; and (4) there is no significant difference in the rate of endogamy between Barbadians who have returned to Barbados and those who have stayed in New York.

0555.  "Number of West Indians Living in New York City Rapidly Increasing." New York Times (June 12, 1974), p. 47.

0556.  Palmer, Ransford W. "A Decade of West Indian Migration to the United States, 1962-1972: An Economic Analysis." Social and Economic Studies, Vol. 23, No. 4 (December 1974), pp. 571-587.

U.S. immigration policy since 1965, by giving preference to skilled and educated workers, has caused the increasing immigration of trained individuals from the West Indies. Through a case study of Jamaica, this article argues that the emigration of workers is a function of the wage differential between Jamaica and the U.S. It concludes that, in the absence of larger change, higher wages in the U.S. will continue to exert a strong pull on available skilled individuals in Jamaica and the West Indies generally.

0557.  Peck, James J. H. "The Proud West Indian." Our World, Vol. 5, No. 1 (January 1950), pp. 11-18.

0558.  Ramidar, Frankie. "Low Assimilation of Trinidadian Immigrants in American Life." M.A. thesis, Hunter College, 1976.

0559.  Raphael, L. "To Be or Not To Be an American Negro." Negro Digest, Vol. 13 (November 1963), pp. 30-34.

0560.  Raphael, Lennox. "West Indians and Afro-Americans." Freedomways, Vol. 4, No. 3 (Summer 1964), pp. 438-445.

Compared to Black Americans, Afro-West Indians have enjoyed more civil rights. They are hence more assertive and aggressive. Most of the West Indians in the U.S. are of middle-class background and are more motivated toward ambition, education, and pride. They often see Black Americans as lacking these three virtues. This perception of difference results in the lack of unity between the two groups in their struggles for better lives.

0561. Record, Wilson. "The Garvey Movement." Journal of Negro Education, Vol. 25, No. 4 (1956).

0562. Reid, Ira de A. "Race, Migration, and Citizenship: An Essay on the Inter-relations of the West Indian Negro and the United States Negro." In The Negro in the Americas. Ed., Charles H. Wesley. Washington, DC: Graduate School Division of the Social Sciences, Howard University, pp. 55-71.

0563. Sackey, J. A. "The Migration of High Level Personnel from Guyana: Toward an Alternative Analysis." Transition, Vol. 1, No. 1 (1978), pp. 45-48.

0564. Samuels, Wilfred David. "Five Afro-Caribbean Voices in American Culture, 1917 - 1929: Hubert H. Harrison, Wilfred A. Domingo, Richard B. Moore, Cyril V. Briggs, and Claude McKay." Ph.D. dissertation, University of Iowa, 1977. 181 pp. (DAI: 38/07A, p. 4234)

This dissertation examines the dominant theses, programs, and pronounce-ments of the five West Indian immigrant activists. Their thoughts and activities are assessed with reference to the plights and struggles of Black Americans during the Progressive Era.

0565. Smith, Shirley Jeanne. "Industrial Growth, Employment Opportunities, and Migration Within and From Jamaica, 1943-1970." Ph.D. Dissertation, University of Pennsylvania, 1975. (DAI: 36/12A, p. 8331)

The dramatic economic growth of Jamaica during the period had not brought comparable advantage to the population at large. The population growth was moderated by extensive population movement, both internal and external. The 1950s and early 1960s witnessed massive emigration to Great Britain. The late 1960s were a period of massive movement to the U.S. This study shows that emigrants are more responsive to economic factors.

0566. Sowell, Thomas. "The Other Blacks: I and II." New York Times (April 12, 1979), p. A23; (April 13, 1979), p. A27.

0567. Spurling, John J. "Social Relationships Between American Negroes and West Indian Negroes in a Long Island Community: An Explanatory Examination of Intragroup Relationships in the Addisleigh Park Neighborhood of St. Albans, Long Island, New York." Ph. D. dissertation, New York University, 1962. (DAI: 23/06A, p. 2244)

This study is based on interviews with 40 wives of American Black families and 40 wives of West Indian Black families living in the Addisleigh Park neighborhood. It finds that there is little social interrelationship existing between the two groups of families. Furthermore, length of residence, socio-economic status, education, and proximity of residence to members of the opposite group do not operate to produce cross-group association in this community.

0568. Sutton, Constance R. and Makiesky, Susan R. "Migration and West Indian Racial and Ethnic Consciousness." In Migration and Development. Eds., H. I. Safa and B. M. Du Toit. The Hague: Mouton, 1975, pp. 113-144.

The authors observe a change in the content of group and political consciousness among Barbadian immigrants in England and the U.S.  Earlier the Barbadians
tended to emphasize an ethnic identity based on national origin.  After the
mid-1960s there was a shift toward heightened racial consciousness and
pride in blackness.  This development merged with other Third World movements
in opposition to Western hegemony.  Finally, there was also a parallel change
in Barbados itself; and the two-way influences in the raising of racial
consciousness between emigrants abroad and their home country is emphasized
by the authors.

0569.  Tobias, Peter M.  "'How You Gonna Keep Em Down in the Tropics Once
They've Dreamed New York?': Some Aspects of Grenadian Immigration."  Ph.D.
dissertation, Rice University, 1975.  240 pp. (DAI: 36/04A, p. 2300)

This case study of Grenadian migration questions the basic assumptions of
the "push-pull" hypothesis.  Among Grenadians, economic factors, or any one
set of factors, do not invariably lead individuals to become migrants.  An
alternative model is proposed which treats Grenadian migration as one of
many cases in which information must be created and transmitted by actors
who have a pragmatic interest in a particular outcome.  Social interactions
in which such information is transmitted are examined.

0570.  Ueda, Reed.  "West Indians."  In Harvard Encyclopedia of American Ethnic
Groups.  Ed., Stephen Thernstrom.  Cambridge: Harvard University Press, 1980,
pp. 1020-1027.

0571.  Walter, John C.  "Black Immigrants and Political Radicalism in the Harlem
Renaissance."  The Western Journal of Black Studies, Vol. 1, No. 2 (June 1977),
pp. 131-141.

The Harlem Renaissance is not merely an artistic revival, but also a radical
political movement impregnated with Black nationalistic strivings.  A number
of Black immigrants from the West Indies played vital roles in this movement
and found release for their frustrations in it.  This paper analyzes the backgrounds, ideologies, and activities of these immigrant leaders and the legacy
they left behind.

0572.  Walter, John C.  "West Indian Immigrants: Those Arrogant Bastards."
Contributions in Black Studies, No. 5 (1981-82), pp. 17-27.

Describes the achievements and self-pride of West Indian immigrants, and
native Afro-Americans' resentment toward them.  Both immigrants and
natives are to be blamed for the tension between the two groups.

0573.  Watson, Hilbourne A.  "International Migration and the Political Economy
of Underdevelopment: Aspects of the Commonwealth Caribbean Situation."  In
Caribbean Migration to the United States.  Eds., R. S. Bryce-Laporte and D.  M.
Mortimer.  Washington, DC: Smithsonian Institution, Research Institute on Immigration and Ethnic Studies, Occasional Papers No. 1, 1976, pp. 16-43.

0574.  White, Noel.  "The Contribution of West Indian Immigrants to the Negro
Community in the U.S."  M.A. thesis, Columbia University Teachers College,
1968.

0575.  Williams, Katherine.  Where Else But America?  Vignettes on American
Life by a West Indian Female Immigrant.  Annapolis, MD: Fishergate Publishing,
1977.

# 4.
# Cubans in the United States

0576. Adessa, Dominick J. "Refugee Cuban Children: The Role of the Catholic Welfare Bureau of the Diocese of Miami, Florida in Receiving, Caring for and Placing Unaccompanied Cuban Children." M.S.W. thesis, Fordham University, 1964.

0577. Aguirre, Benigno E. "Differential Migration of Cuban Social Races: A Review and Interpretation of the Problems." Latin American Research Review, Vol. 11, No. 1 (1976), pp. 103-124.

> While Cuban emigrants have been mostly Whites, Blacks have participated less and less in the exodus. Three factors are seen to underlie this differential migration: (1) Cuban Blacks have considerably improved their social and economic conditions after the Revolution; (2) they tend to have fewer relatives who have already migrated to the U.S.; and (3) political ideology tends to encourage them to stay and participate in the Cuban revolutionary construction.

0578. Aguirre, B. E. "The Marital Stability of Cubans in the United States." Ethnicity, Vol. 8, No. 4 (December 1981), pp. 387-405.

> A statistical analysis of factors affecting the stability of different Cuban marriage types differentiated along three dimensions: marriage contracted in Cuba or the U.S.; marriage contracted before or after the Revolution; whether the marriage contractor came to the U.S. before or after the Revolution.

0579. Aguirre-Lopez, Benigno E. "The Marital Stability of Cuban Immigrants: 1970." Ph.D. dissertation, Ohio State University, 1977. 210 pp. (DAI: 38/08A, p. 5067)

> This study is based on a five percent public-use national sample of the 1970 Census. Eight immigrant marriage types are identified. Findings indicate that the marital stability of men increases with higher cultural and social origins and with greater personal resources. The marital stability of women decreases with increasing instrumental ability and is enhanced by greater family resources and integration. These findings are related to the disrupting effects of immigration on traditional marriage system.

0580. Alexander, T. "Those Amazing Cuban Emigres." Fortune (October 1966), pp. 144-149.

Although many of them are working at jobs that are beneath their qualifications, Cuban immigrants are making it economically and becoming an important American asset.

0581. Alum, Rolando and Alum, Luis A. "On the Assimilation of Cuban Exiles." International Migration Review, Vol. 12, No. 1 (Spring 1978), pp. 143-144.

0582. Alvarez, C. M. and Pader, O. F. "Locus of Control Among Anglo-Americans and Cuban-Americans." Journal of Social Psychology, Vol. 105 (August 1978), pp. 195-198.

This comparative study suggests that age, and not necessarily ethnicity, is a deciding factor in determining perceptions of an internal or an external locus of control. Older Cuban-Americans are found to score higher on internal perception of locus control due to the fact that they actually enacted personal choices, such as emigrating from their country.

0583. Alvarez, C. M. and Pader, O. F. "Co-operative and Competitive Behavior of Cuban-American and Anglo-American Children." Journal of Psychology, Vol. 101 (March 1979), pp. 265-271.

This study compares two groups of Cuban-American children and a group of Anglo-American children in their performance on the Madsen Cooperation Board. Under group reward instructions, all three groups demonstrated their ability to perform cooperatively. Under individual reward instructions, all groups decreased in cooperation, but the Anglo-American group was the only group to maintain a significant level of competitiveness.

0584. Arguelles, Lourdes. "Cuban Political Refugees in the United States: A Study of Social Mobility and Authoritarianism." Ph.D. dissertation, New York University, 1970. 145 pp. (DAI: 31/05A, p. 2491)

This study examines the authoritarian proclivities of Cuban emigres, and relates them to social mobility patterns and other crucial variables in the assimilation process. Data show that social mobility, political behavior, degree of assimilation, and education have significant relationships to authoritarianism.

0585. Arguelles, Lourdes. "The U.S. National Security State: The CIA and Cuban Emigre Terrorism." Race and Class, Vol. 23, No. 4 (Spring 1982), pp. 287-304.

Describes Cuban emigres' involvement in paramilitary and terrorist activities. The sponsorship and support of emigre terrorism by the national security establishment is examined.

0586. Arguelles, Lourdes. "Cuban Miami: The Roots, Development, Everyday Life of an Emigre Enclave in the U.S. National Security State." Contemporary Marxism, No. 5 (Summer 1982), pp. 27-43.

This paper examines the structure through which Cuban emigres have "historically performed roles at the behest of the American ruling class." The political-economic matrix of Miami's Cuban community is described in a detailed account of the Cubans' involvement in drug traffic, organized crime, and covert intelligence operations. The community's structure and norms are reproduced through the emigre elite's control of the media and manipulation of social service programs.

0587. Arguelles, Lourdes and MacEoin, Gary. The Cubans in the U.S.: Revolution, Displacement and Terror. New York: Holt, Rinehart and Winston, forthcoming.

0588. Azicri, Max. "The Politics of Exile: Trends and Dynamics of Political Change Among Cuban-Americans." Cuban Studies, Vol. 11, No. 2/Vol. 12, No. 1, (July, 1981/January, 1982), pp. 55-73.

The changes in political values and attitudes of Cuban-Americans are examined through four periods: (1) the 1960s, characterized by anti-Castro political activism; (2) 1970-77, development of political pluralism with the emergence of progressive political attitudes; (3) 1978-79, dominated by the dialogue and massive visits of Cuban-Americans to the Island; and (4) 1980-81, revival of political conservatism under the impact of the Mariel boatlift and the election of Reagan. Throughout the periods, the political cleavages within the Cuban community are explained as the result of the unevenness in cultural and structural assimilation.

0589. Azicri, Max, ed. Cuban-Americans in the 1980s: The Present Outlook of a New Minority. Forthcoming.

0590. Bach, Robert L. "The New Cuban Immigrants: Their Background and Prospects." Monthly Labor Review, Vol. 103, No. 10 (October 1980), pp. 39-46.

The 1980 Cuban refugees were mostly young working-age men; their education and skill levels were above average for Cuba; and the number of ex-offenders among them was significant but included many jailed for political reasons.

0591. Bach, Robert L. "The New Cuban Exodus: Political and Economic Motivations." Caribbean Review, Vol. 11, No. 1 (Winter 1982), pp. 22-25, 58-60.

Presents brief social background profiles of Cuban refugees arriving during the Mariel boatlifts. Pejorative labels given to this group of Cubans such as "social dregs" and "undesirables" are found to be invalid. The author contends that the distinction between economic migrants and political refugees according to individual motivations is misleading. The cause of the Mariel exodus is analyzed in the context of recent Cuban political and economic crises. The ambiguous U.S. reaction to this migration flow is seen as constrained by an economic conservatism on the one hand, and a liberalism in foreign policy on the other.

0592. Bach, Robert L.; Bach, Jennifer B. and Triplett, Timothy. "The Flotilla 'Entrants': Latest and Most Controversial." Cuban Studies, Vol 11, No. 2/Vol. 12, No. 1, (July 1981/January, 1982), pp. 29-48.

Using samples of the Flotilla entrants in Miami and in the camps, this study attempts to present a biographical profile of the 1980 Cuban refugees. Compared to all preceding waves of Cuban exiles, this group is found to be younger, has a greater proportion of Blacks and mulattoes, and comes from more diverse geographical origins. Most of the entrants were actively employed, and were neither marginal to the Cuban economy nor outside of the social mainstream. Only a small proportion of them can be called "social dregs."

0593. Baloyra, Enrique A. "Comment - Making Waves: A View of the Cuban Community in the U.S." Cuban Studies, Vol. 11, No. 2/Vol. 12, No. 1 (July 1981/-January 1982), pp. 75-78.

0594. Bastista, Laureano F. "Political Sociology of the Cuban Exile, 1959-1968." M.A. thesis, University of Miami, 1969.

0595. Bender, Lynn D. "The Cuban Exiles: An Analytical Sketch." Journal of Latin American Studies, Vol. 5, No. 2 (November 1973), pp. 271-278.

A short sketch of the major waves of Cuban immigration between 1961 and 1972. Briefly discusses the socioeconomic characteristics and political orientations of Cuban immigrants.

0596. Bernardo, Benes. The Impact of Cuban Exiles on the Economy of South Florida. Miami: Economic Society of South Florida, 1971.

0597. Boone, Margaret S. "Social Structure of a Low-Density Cultural Group: Cubans in Washington, D.C." Anthropological Quarterly, Vol. 54 (April 1981), pp. 103-109.

0598. Boone, Margaret S. "The Use of Traditional Concepts in the Development of New Urban Roles: Cuban Women in the United States." In A World of Women. Ed., Erika Bourguignon. New York: Praeger, 1980.

0599. Bourne, Richard. "The Cubans of Miami." New Society, (August 8, 1974), pp. 347-350.

0600. Bracker, M. "Better, Frustrated, Divided: Cuba's Refugees." New York Times Magazine (April 21, 1963), p. 7.

0601. Burkholz, Herbert. "The Latinization of Miami." New York Times Magazine (September 21, 1980), pp. 45-47, 84, 86, 88, 98, 100.

The influx of Cuban immigrants has made Miami "the capital of Latin America." At the same time when it has become a financial heaven for Latin Americans, it has also become an economic hell for its own Blacks. The May 1980 riot in Liberty City is put in the context of Black resentment and protest.

0602. Carballo, M. "A Socio-Psychological Study of Acculturation-Assimilation: Cubans in New Orleans." Ph.D. dissertation, Tulane University, 1970. 347 pp. (DAI: 31/06A, p. 3053)

This dissertation, based on a study of 192 Cuban refugees in New Orleans, argues that acculturation and assimilation are two distinctive stages in the overall process of post-migration adjustment. A number of socio-psychological variables are examined to help determine the character of these different stages.

0603. Casal, Lourdes. "Cubans in the U.S." Nueva Generacion, No. 3-4 (December 1972), pp. 6-20.

0604. Casal, Lourdes. "Cubans in the U.S.: Their Impact on U.S.-Cuba Relations." In Revolutionary Cuba in the World Arena. Ed., Martin Weinstein. Philadelphia: ISHI Publications (Institute for the Study of Human Issues), 1979, pp. 109-136.

0605. Casal, Lourdes and Prieto, Yolanda. "Black Cubans in the United States: Basic Demographic Information." In Female Immigrants to the United States. Eds., D. M. Mortimer and R. S. Bryce-Laporte. Washington, DC: Smithsonian Institution, Research Institute for Ethnic Studies, Occasional Papers No. 2, 1981, pp. 314-348.

  Presents statistical data on some characteristics of Black Cubans in the United States, including employment, education, and income. Also discusses the socio-psychological characteristics of a Dade County Black Cuban sample with special emphasis on Black Cuban females. Comparisons between Black and White Cubans are given.

0606. Clark, Juan M. "The Cuban Escapees as Possible Factual Indicators." Latinamericanist, (November 1, 1970), pp. 1-4.

0607. Clark, Juan M. "The Exodus from Revolutionary Cuba (1959-1974): A Sociological Analysis." Ph.D. dissertation, University of Florida, 1975. 288 pp. (DAI: 36/12A, p. 8307)

  This study discusses the conditions of Cuban emigration, its magnitude, and its periodization. It also describes the situations of refugees, their socio-demographic characteristics, and how these characteristics compare to those of the parent Cuban population.

0608. Clark, Juan M. Why? The Cuban Exodus: Background, Evolution, and Impact in U.S.A. Miami: Union of Cubans in Exile, 1977. 36 pp.

0609. Clark, Juan M. The 1980 Mariel Exodus: An Assessment and Prospect. Washington, DC: Council for Inter-American Security, 1981. 21 pp.

0610. Clark, Juan M.; Lasaga, Jose I. and Reque, Rose S. The 1980 Mariel Exodus: An Assessment and Prospect. A Special Report. Washington, DC: Council for Inter-American Security, 1981. 21 pp.

0611. Clark, Juan M. et al. Hispanics in Dade County: Their Characteristics and Needs. Dade County, FL: Office of the County Manager, Latin Affairs, 1980. 73 pp.

0612. Conaway, James. "Unwanted Immigrants: Cuban Prisons in America." Atlantic, Vol. 247, No. 2 (February 1981), pp. 72-81.

  A journalistic account of the author's visit to Fort Chaffee. Contains some of his interviews with the Cuban refugees.

0613. Cooney, Rosemary S. and Contreras, Maria A. "Residence Patterns of Social Register Cubans: A Study of Miami, San Juan, and New York SMSAs." Cuban Studies, Vol. 8, No. 2 (1978), pp. 33-50.

  This study compares the residence patterns of Cuban elites listed in Social Register in the three cities. The degrees of segregation of these Cubans from other Cubans and from other upper-middle-class communities are examined.

0614. Cortes, Carlos E., ed. Cuban Exiles in the United States: An Original Anthology. New York: Arno Press, 1980.

0615. Cortes, Carlos E., ed. The Cuban Experience in the United States: An Original Anthology. New York: Arno Press, 1980.

0616. Cortes, Carlos E., ed. Cuban Refugee Programs: An Original Anthology. New York: Arno Press, 1980.

0617. Cortes, Carlos E., ed. Cuban Minority in the United States. New York: Arno Press, 1981. 2 vols.

0618. "Cuban Refugees: The Preferred Minority." Sepia, Vol. 19, No. 10 (October 1970), pp. 8-13.

  Argues that the Cuban refugee airlifts of the 1960s were a waste of taxpayer's money. The Cubans in the U.S. are taking money and jobs needed by Blacks, while the latter continue to suffer poverty. They are causing many problems in their cities of concentration such as Miami.

0619. Cuban Resource Center. "Cuban Exiles in the United States." Cuban Resource Center Newsletter, Vol. 2, No. 4 (July 1972).

0620. Cuban Studies. Vol. 11, No. 2/Vol 12, No. 1 (July 1981/January 1982), "The Cuban Exodus: A Symposium."

0621. Daly, Michael. "Los Bandidos Take the Town." New York, Vol. 14 (October 26, 1981), pp. 67-73.

0622. Diaz, Guarione M., ed. Evaluation and Identification of Policy Issues in the Cuban Community. Miami: Cuban National Planning Council, 1981. 190 pp.

  On social conditions of and social service for Cubans in Miami and Union City, New York.

0623. Dixon, Heriberto. "Who Ever Heard of a Black Cuban?" Afro-Hispanic Review, Vol. 1, No. 3 (September 1982), pp. 10-12.

  Black Cubans are underrepresented in the major areas of Cuban settlement in the U.S. and constitute an invisible sector of the general Cuban community. The author calls for more empirical studies of the relationships existing among Black Cubans and other social/ethnic groups.

0624. Dominguez, Virginia. "The Nature of Change: Cuban Women in the United States." In Women and Change: The Cuban Case. Ed., Maria Cristina Herrera. Institute of Cuban Studies, 1981.

0625. Dowd, Donald Jerome. "A Comparative Study of Attitudes, Goals and Values Between Negro American, White American, and Cuban Refugee Groups in a Large Southern City." Ed.D. dissertation, University of Florida, 1966. 120 pp. (DAI: 27/10A, p. 3306)

  This is a study of 96 students from two high schools in Dade County, Florida. The three subgroups are compared in terms of their attitudes and values held, and their goals sought. Specific aspects examined include the groups' respective perceptions of their neighborhood, school, career expectation, friendship, and family. Of the three groups, the Cubans tend to have the most positive perception of the distance from desired goals.

0626. Egerton, John. Cubans in Miami: A Third Dimension in Racial and Cultural Relations. Nashville: Race Relations Information Center, Special Report, 1969. 26 pp.

A study based on interviews of Cuban-Black relations and Cubans' acceptance by the White majority. Although the interests of Cubans and Blacks in Miami tend to coincide, a coalition does not seem imminent.

0627. Fagen, Richard and Brody, Richard A. "Cubans in Exile: A Demographic Analysis." Social Problems, VoL 2 (1964), pp. 389-401.

Compares the demographic characteristics of Cuban refugees to those of the home population (1953 Census data), with discussion on changes over time among early refugees.

0628. Fagen, Richard; Brody, R. A. and O'Leary, R. J. Cubans in Exile: Disaffection and the Revolution. Stanford: Stanford University Press, 1968. 161 pp.

0629. Fernandez, Gaston A. "Comment - The Flotilla Entrants: Are They Different?" Cuban Studies, VoL 11, No. 2/VoL 12, No. 1 (July 1981/January 1982), pp. 49-54.

0630. Ferree, M. M. "Employment Without Liberation: Cuban Women in the United States." Social Science Quarterly, VoL 60 (July 1979), pp. 35-50.

0631. Fox, Geoffrey E. Working-Class Emigres From Cuba. Palo Alto: R & E Research Associates, 1979.

0632. Gallagher, Patrick Lee. The Cuban Exile: A Socio-Political Analysis. New York: Arno Press, 1980.

0633. Garzon, C. C. "A Study of the Adjustment of 34 Cuban Boys in Exile." M.S.W. thesis, Florida State University, 1965.

0634. Gibboney, J. "Stability and Change in Components of Parental Role Among Cuban Refugees." Ph.D. dissertation, Catholic University of America, 1967. 272 pp. (DAI: 28/07A, p. 2799)

This study is based on questionnaire surveys of and interviews with Cuban fathers in Washington, D.C., Baltimore, and Columbus, Ohio. The data reveal a consistent relationship between the degree of parental role change, as measured by the extent to which the parents participate in child-care and household activities, and change in three aspects of the sociological situations within the family: (1) change in the presence or absence of extended family members; (2) change in mother's work status; and (3) change in the socioeconomic status of the family.

0635. Gil, Rosa Maria. "The Assimilation and Problems of 100 Cuban Refugees Attending Catholic and Public High Schools in Union City and West New York, New Jersey: 1959-1966." M.S.W. thesis, Fordham University, 1968.

0636. Gil, Vincent E. "The Personal Adjustment and Acculturation of Cuban Immigrants in Los Angeles." Ph.D. dissertation, University of California, Los Angeles, 1976. 349 pp. (DAI: 37/01A, p. 423)

This ethnographic study investigates the social-psychological factors related to the Cuban's personal adjustment and acculturation. Data from adjustment and acculturation scales show that the Cuban emigre has achieved a high measure of personal adjustment, and a moderate level of acculturation. Economically and occupationally, the Cuban has surpassed median Los Angeles

County levels for both Anglo and Spanish-surnamed individuals. The processes of the Cuban's adjustment and acculturation are largely conditioned by internal-motivational determinants, not, as has been assumed, the external dimensions of Anglo life.

0637.  Haskins, James. The New Americans: Cuban Boat People. New York: Enslow Publications, 1982. 64 pp.

0638.  Hernandez, Andres R., ed. The Cuban Minority in the United States: Final Report on Need Identification and Program Evaluation. Washington, DC: Cuban National Planning Council, 1974. 321 pp.

0639.  Hoeffel, Paul Heath. "Fort Chaffee's Unwanted Cubans." The New York Times Magazine (December 21, 1980), pp. 30, 42, 44, 47, 50, 52, 54.

Describes the hardship and frustrations of Cuban refugees at Fort Chaffee.

0640.  Joyner, G. C. "The Role of the Family in the Adjustment of Cuban Refugees." M.A. thesis, University of Florida, 1972.

0641.  Kandel, Randy Frances and Heider, Marion. "Friendship and Factionalism in a Tri-ethnic Housing Complex for the Elderly in North Miami." Anthropological Quarterly, Vol. 52, No. 1 (January 1979), pp. 49-59.

This article analyzes the impact of ethnicity, architectural design, and internal politics on community formation in a housing complex for Black, Cuban, and Anglo elderly. It is found that within the complex ethnic and residential boundaries separating the three groups are recognized in the formation of social groups.

0642.  Lanier, Alfredo S. "Give Me Your Tired, Your Poor... And the Cubans Came: But Are They Better Off?" Chicago Magazine, Vol. 29 (September 1980), pp. 152-155.

0643.  "The Latinization of Miami." Price Waterhouse Review, Vol. 22, No. 1 (1977), pp. 6, 8, 11-14, 16-17.

0644.  Levine, Barry B. "Sources of Ethnic Identity for Latin Florida: Cubans in Miami." Caribbean Review, Vol. 8, No. 1 (January-March 1979), pp. 30-34.

0645.  Linehan, Edward J. "Cuban Exiles Bring New Life to Miami." National Geographic, Vol. 144 (July, 1973), pp. 68-95.

0646.  Llanes, Jose. Cuban-Americans: Masters of Survival. Cambridge: Abt Books, 1982. 229 pp.

0647.  Lopez Blanco, M.; Montiel, P. A. and Suarez, L. L. "A Study of Attitudes of Cuban Refugees Toward Assimilation: Selected Attitudes of Cuban Refugees in the Miami Area." M.S.W. thesis, Barry College, 1968.

0648.  Mackey, William F. and Beebe, Von N. Bilingual Schools for a Bicultural Community: Miami's Adaptation to the Cuban Refugees. Rowley, MA: Newbury House, 1977.

0649.  Maier, Francis X. and McColm, R. Bruce. "Nation in Our Midst: The Cuban Diaspora." National Review, Vol. 33, No. 3 (February 20, 1981), pp. 148-150, 152, 184.

Describes the efforts and strategies of the Cuban exile community to over-throw Castro.

0650. Mayer, J. C. "Women Without Men: Selected Attitudes of Some Cuban Refugees." M.A. thesis, University of Florida, 1966.

0651. McCaughan, Ed. "Causes of Immigration from Socialist Cuba." Contemporary Marxism, No. 5 (Summer 1982), pp. 44-47.

The major causes of Cuban immigration are the difficulties of development and socialist construction within a hostile environment of the capitalist world-system. Immigration from Cuba also serves political and propagandistic functions for U.S. foreign policy.

0652. McColm, R. Bruce and Maier, Francis X. "Fighting Castro from Exile." New York Times Magazine (January 4, 1981), pp. 28-30, 32, 34-35, 38, 40.

The anti-Castro consensus in the Cuban exile community has been significantly bolstered by new waves of refugees. However, the community has also been infiltrated by Castro's agents.

0653. McCoy, Clyde B.; Page, J. Brian and Gonzalez, Diana H. "Cuban and Other Latin Immigration to Florida." In Florida Economic Indicators. Gainesville: Bureau of Economic and Business Research, University of Florida.

0654. Mesa, Jose Luis. "Intra-Urban Residential Mobility and Ethnicity: Cuban-Americans in Lansing, Michigan." Ph.D. dissertation, Michigan State University, 1978.  138 pp. (DAI: 39/03A, p. 1836)

This study in social geography examines the spatial patterns of intra-urban residential mobility among Cuban-Americans in Lansing during the period 1963-76. Findings support three main propositions: (1) a "receptor" residential area has functioned as a focus of Cuban residential activity; (2) relocations of ethnic groups, including Cubans, to suburban areas reflect a clustered spatial structure, indicating the importance of ethnic bonds; and (3) ethnic channels of information have significantly influenced the selection of residential location.

0655. Miyares, Javier. "Cuban-Americans: Who Are They?" NCCA News (National Center for Community Action), No. 1 (July 1978), pp. 1-4.

0656. Miyares, Javier and Perez-Lopez, Jorge. "Florida's Cuban-Americans' Participation in the Electoral Process." NCCA News (National Center for Community Action), No. 3-4 (September-October 1978), pp. 1-3.

0657. Moncarz Percal, R. "A Study of the Effect of Environmental Change on Human Capital Among Selected Skilled Cubans." Ph.D. dissertation, Florida State University, 1969.  341 pp. (DAI: 30/11A, p. 4635)

This study analyzes the utilization or underutilization of occupational skills among various groups of Cuban immigrants since 1959. It finds that adaptation has been complete for the civil engineers, electrical engineers, and architects, while for all the other occupation groups full adaptation has not been attained due to professional and legal restrictions.

0658. Moncarz Percal, Raul. "Professional Adaptation of the Cuban Teachers in the United States, 1959-1969." International Migration, Vol 8 (1970), pp. 110-116.

0659. Moncarz Percal, Raul. "Professional Adaptation of Cuban Physicians in the United States, 1959-1969." International Migration News, Vol 4 (Spring 1970), pp. 80-86.

0660. Moncarz Percal, Raul. "The Golden Cage: Cubans in Miami." International Migration, Vol 16, No. 3/4 (1978), pp. 160-173.

This study examines the Cubans' adjustment process and its scope in terms of educational, geographical, and income mobility. Findings indicate that in terms of educational mobility, the loss of human capital has been very significant. The Cubans' geographical mobility out of Florida is ineffective. Finally, in terms of income and occupation, there is downward mobility. This study challenges the validity of generalizations about Cuban success stories.

0661. Morgan, Ivette de Arteaga. "Factors Affecting Acculturation of Cuban Refugee Students in Miami." D.A. dissertation, University of Miami, 1977. 124 pp. (DAI: 38/04A, p. 1959)

Study based on a sample drawn from students at a small private college in Miami. The effects of sex, age, and length of residence in the U.S. on the level of acculturation are explored. Major findings include: (1) women have a faster rate of acculturation; (2) age is an important factor in degree of acculturation for females but not for males; (3) years in the U.S. is an important factor in acculturation for females but not for males.

0662. Morrison, A. "Miami's Cuban Refugee Crisis." Ebony, Vol 18 (July 1960), pp. 96-100.

0663. Moscowitz, Daniel B. "Prisoners of Circumstance: The Cuban Problem." Corrections Magazine, Vol 6 (December 1980), pp. 42-47.

0664. New York Times. "Why Castro Exports Cubans." November 7, 1965, pp. 30 ff.

0665. New York Times. "Admission to U.S. of Cuban Refugees Who Have Settled in Other Countries." April 23, 1972, p. 15.

0666. Oettinger, K. "Services to Unaccompanied Cuban Refugee Children in the U.S." Social Services Review, Vol 36 (December 1962), pp. 337-384.

0667. Page, J. Bryan. "The Children of Exile: Relationships Between the Acculturation Process and Drug Use Among Cuban Youth." Youth and Society, Vol 11, No. 4 (June 1980) pp. 431-447.

This ethnographic study is based on information gathered in the Miami area. The drug use patterns among Cuban youth represent a recombination of elements from the youth subculture of the U.S. and from pre-revolutionary Cuban traditions. The youth have derived their alternatives from both cultures.

0668. Pedraza-Bailey, Silvia. "Cubans and Mexicans in the United States: The Functions of Political and Economic Migration." Cuban Studies, VoL 11, No. 2/VoL 12, No. 1, (July 1981/January 1982), pp. 79-97.

The greater success of Cuban immigrants as compared to Mexican immigrants can only be partially explained by the former group's higher social class of origin. The author argues that it is also the result of differential treatment by the U.S. government. Cubans as political immigrants have been given a generous reception and substantial assistance by the state. In contrast, Mexicans are economic immigrants whom the state has made little attempt to assist.

0669. Perez, Lisandro. "Cubans." In Harvard Encyclopedia of American Ethnic Groups. Ed., Stephen Thernstrom. Cambridge: Harvard University Press, 1980, pp. 256-261.

0670. Perez, Louis A., Jr. "Cubans in Tampa: From Exiles to Immigrants, 1892-1901." Florida Historical Quarterly, VoL 57 (October 1978), pp. 129-140.

0671. Philipson, Lorrin and Llerena, Rafael. Freedom Flights: Cuban Refugees Talk About Life Under Castro and How They Fled His Regime. New York: Random House, 1981. 201 pp.

0672. Portes, Alejandro. "Dilemmas of a Golden Exile: Integration of Cuban Refugee Families in Milwaukee." American Sociological Review, VoL 34, No. 4 (August 1969), pp. 505-518.

Cubans who fled the Revolution are mostly of upper and middle social strata. This paper examines their integration as a fundamental shift from psychological attachments to their past in Cuba to values and identities congruent with the new environment. It is found that integration is strongly influenced by relative level of present socioeconomic reward. These findings are interpreted as related to the rational-individualistic ethic characterizing families from these formerly dominant sectors of Cuba.

0673. Portes, Alejandro. Immigrants' Attainment: An Analysis of Occupation and Earnings Among Cuban Exiles in the United States. Durham: Duke University, Center for International Studies, Occasional Papers Series, 1980. 26 pp.

0674. Portes, Alejandro and Bach, Robert L. "Immigrant Earnings: Cuban and Mexican Immigrants in the United States." International Migration Review, VoL 14, No. 3 (Fall 1980), pp. 315-340.

This study examines the determinants of earnings among recent Cuban and Mexican immigrants interviewed at the time of arrival and reinterviewed three years later. The findings suggest that the phenomenon of immigrant economic enclaves represents an important qualification to general predictions based on segmented labor markets.

0675. Portes, A.; Clark, J. M. and Bach, R. L. "The New Wave: A Statistical Profile of Recent Cuban Exiles to the U.S." Cuban Studies, VoL 7, No. 1 (January 1977), pp. 1-32.

This paper presents a statistical profile of 590 male Cubans coming to the U.S. during late 1973 and early 1974. The profile includes dimensions which are relevant for the immigrants' future adjustment such as objective qualifications and skills, and subjective aspirations and personality traits.

0676. Portes Alejandro; Clark, Juan M. and Lopez, Manuel M. "Six Years Later, The Process of Incorporation of Cuban Exiles in the United States: 1973-1979." Cuban Studies, Vol. 11, No. 2/Vol. 12, No. 1 (July 1981/January 1982), pp. 1-24.

The article presents results from a six-year longitudinal study of Cuban exiles. A sample of 590 male Cubans were interviewed in Miami in 1973; reinterviewed in 1976; and again in 1979. Four general areas are examined: (1) residential patterns; (2) education, knowledge, and information; (3) attitudes toward self and toward the host society; and (4) employment and income. Findings reveal that, due to the unique context of an economic enclave created by earlier exiles, the process of incorporation of Cubans does not fit the predictions of the consensus-based assimilation theory, nor does it entirely agree with the conflict-based internal colony perspective. Characteristics of the enclave formation are: (1) the growth and visible presence of immigrant enterprises and (2) the fact that the average immigrant does not have to go beyond the enclave to meet his/her needs.

0677. Portes, Alejandro; McLeod, Samuel A., Jr. and Parker, Robert N. "Immigrant Aspirations." Sociology of Education, Vol. 51, No. 4 (October 1978), pp. 241-260.

This paper examines the nature and determinants of occupational, income, and educational aspirations among Mexican and Cuban immigrants surveyed in 1973. Their aspirations are compared with actual attainments of labor force participants both in their countries of origin and in the U.S. Through regression analysis, aspirations are found to be governed by rational assessment of objective opportunities, as determined by the individual's past experiences of educational, occupational, and income attainment, and the objective ability to speak the language of the host society. On the other hand, individual attitudes and personality variables have little effect on the level of aspiration.

0678. Portes, A.; Parker, R. N. and Cobas, J. A. "Assimilation or Consciousness: Perceptions of U.S. Society Among Recent Latin American Immigrants to the United States." Social Forces, Vol. 59, No. 1 (September 1980), pp. 200-224.

Two views of immigrants' perceptions of U.S. society and discrimination are compared and tested. As immigrants gain greater familiarity with the culture and language and some economic advancement, the assimilation theory predicts they will have a more favorable evaluation of the host society, while conflict theories suggest they will be more critical in their overall assessment. These competing hypotheses are statistically tested on samples of Cuban and Mexican immigrants and the results support conflict theories.

0679. Prohias, Rafael and Casal, Lourdes. The Cuban Minority in the U.S.: Preliminary Report on Need Identification and Program Evaluation. Boca Raton: Florida Atlantic University, 1974. 445 pp.

A report prepared by the Cuban National Planning Council. It consists of: (1) a review of literature; (2) a demographic study of Cubans; (3) an analysis of their economic adjustment; (4) an evaluation of the needs; (5) a review of assistant programs and the Cubans' participation in them; and (6) policy recommendations.

0680. Reyes, Manolo J. Elderly Cubans in Exile. Washington, DC: U.S. Government Printing Office, 1971. 20 pp. (SuDoc Number: Y4.Ag4:C89)

0681. Richardson, Raipa Carregado. "The Relationship of Ethnic Group Membership, Age, Sex, Achievement and Locus of Control to the Self-Report of a Group of Cuban Students in the University of Florida." Ph.D. dissertation, University of Florida, 1976. 134 pp. (DAI: 37/07A, p. 4243)

> This study of 127 Cuban students finds that they have higher mean scores in self-concept than the American norm group. They are more defensive or reluctant to disclose derogatory information about themselves. No significant relationships are found for them between self-concept on the one hand, and social class, age, length of time in the U.S., academic achievement, and sex on the other.

0682. Richmond, Marie LaLiberte. "Immigrant Adaptation and Family Structure Among Cubans in Miami, Florida." Ph.D. dissertation, Florida State University, 1973. 201 pp. (DAI: 34/10A, p. 6773)

> This study examines the impact of immigrant adaptation on conjugal role relationship and the socialization of children. It is found that the Cuban exile family is generally less male dominated and has less segregated roles than corresponding interactions in traditional Latin American families. Cuban exile children have gained considerably more independence than their Latin American counterparts. These changes are related to various factors such as the length of residence in the U.S., association with Americans, and the working status of the wife.

0683. Richmond, Marie LaLiberte. Immigrant Adaptation and Family Structure Among Cubans in Miami, Florida. New York: Arno Press, 1980.

0684. Rogg, Eleanor M. "The Occupational Adjustment of Cuban Refugees in the West New York, New Jersey Area." Ph.D. dissertation, Fordham University, 1970. 461 pp. (DAI: 31/06A, p. 3060)

> This study is based on a survey of 250 Cuban households in West New York. Findings indicate that the Cubans have created a strong refugee community, which has aided significantly their adjustment to the host society, while slowing their acculturation to a manageable pace. Although most of them have experienced downward occupational mobility, their satisfaction with their work in the U.S. has been high. It is also found that adjustment and acculturation have been easier and more rapid for Cubans from middle class backgrounds than for those from poorer classes.

0685. Rogg, Eleanor M. "The Influence of a Strong Refugee Community on the Economic Adjustment of its Members." International Migration Review, Vol. 5, No. 4 (Winter 1971), pp. 474-481.

> This article analyzes the economic adjustment of Cuban refugees living in West New York, New Jersey. Based on a sample of 250 interviews with the heads of Cuban families, it finds that despite a marked loss of occupation status among Cubans, there is a strong sense of satisfaction. It is argued that the strength of a Cuban community is a crucial factor in favorably influencing the adjustment of its members.

0686. Rogg, Eleanor Meyer. The Assimilation of Cuban Exiles: The Role of Community and Class. New York: Aberdeen Press, 1974. 241 pp.

A sociological study of the Cuban community in West New York, New Jersey, based on interviews conducted in 1968. The author maintains that the formation of a strong Cuban community helps the immigrants to adjust and that Cubans of high and middle socioeconomic strata acculturate faster than those of the low strata.

0687. Rogg, Eleanor Meyer. "Comment—Six Years Later, the Process of Incorporation of Cuban Exiles in the United States: 1973-1979." Cuban Studies, Vol. 11, No. 2/Vol. 12, No. 1 (July 1981/January 1982), pp. 25-28.

0688. Rogg, Eleanor Meyer and Cooney, Rosemary Santana. Adaptation and Adjustment of Cubans: West New York, New Jersey. Monograph No. 5, Hispanic Research Center, Fordham University, 1980. 93 pp.

This study is based on a survey of 300 Cuban families conducted in 1979. The vitality of the Cuban community in West New York is quite strong, as measured by the following indicators: length of residence, common place of origin, extent of primary group interaction, existence of mutual help and support systems, presence of Cuban ethnic organizations and leaders, and similarity of religious beliefs. The relationships between the Cuban community and the larger society are growing, as shown in four major links: occupation, education, government, and recreation. The core of the monograph consists of statistical analyses of the different variables that impact on the adaptation and adjustment of the Cuban migrants. The variables considered include: occupation, education, sex, age of arrival, etc.

0689. Rothchild, John. "Florida: Sunset in the Sunshine State." Rolling Stone, No. 353 (October 1, 1981), pp. 20-23, 101-102.

0690. Rumbaut, R. D. and Rumbaut, R. G. "Family in Exile: Cuban Expatriates in the United States." American Journal of Psychology, Vol. 133, No. 4 (April 1976), pp. 395-399.

This paper examines the situational determinants which have mitigated the severe circumstances of Cuban refugees and made possible the resilience of their families. The most significant factors include: (1) relatively high occupational and educational levels; (2) formation of vigorous ethnic communities; and (3) effectively organized reception by the United States.

0691. Russell, Dick. "Little Havana's Reign of Terror." New Times (New York), Vol. 7 (October 29, 1976), pp. 36-37, 40-45.

0692. Salter, Paul S. and Mings, Robert C. "The Projected Impact of Cuban Settlement on Voting Patterns in Metropolitan Miami, Florida." The Professional Geographer, Vol. 24, No. 2 (1972), pp. 123-131.

Cubans will make up 26% of the Dade County residents by 1975. As they become integrated into the community, they will become increasingly active in political affairs. As they are expected to support anti-Communist and conservative candidates, they will erode Miami's traditional support for more liberal candidates.

0693. Stevenson, J. "Cuban-Americans: New Urban Class." Ph.D. dissertation, Wayne State University, 1973. 192 pp. (DAI: 34/07A, p. 4440)

A sociological study of Cuban-American businessmen in Dade County, Florida, based on interviews conducted in 1972. Assimilation to and acceptance by the dominant society are explored. Race relations between American Blacks and Cuban-Americans are examined, as well as the situations and problems of Cuban-American Blacks and Cuban-American Jews. The author concludes that these Cuban entrepreneurs exhibit many of the political values of those in power; their presence creates a buffer zone between the affluent Whites and the disenfranchised Blacks; and their success helps to reinforce the myth that the American Dream is still alive.

0694. "Storm in Florida Straits." Economist, Vol. 275 (May 3, 1980), pp. 23-24.

0695. Sutton, Horace. "The Curious Intrigues of Cuban Miami." Saturday Review/World (September 11, 1973), pp. 24-31.

0696. Szapocznik, Jose. "Role Conflict Resolution in Cuban Mothers." Ph. D. dissertation, University of Miami, 1977.   177 pp. (DAI: 38/04B, p. 1908)

The purpose of this study is to crossvalidate a theory of role conflict resolution developed by Gross, McEacher and Mason to a population of Cuban mothers. The role of Morality-Expediency (a personality variable), and perceived legitimacy of demands and perceived negative sanctions (two situational variables) in predicting the behavior of Cuban mothers exposed to role conflict situations is studied.

0697. Szapocznik, Jose and Herrera, Maria C., eds. Cuban Americans: Acculturation, Adjustment and the Family. Washington, DC: Coalition of Spanish Speaking Mental Health Organizations, 1979.

0698. Szapocznik, J. et al. "Cuban Value Structure: Treatment Implications." Journal of Consulting and Clinical Psychology, Vol. 46, No. 5 (October 1978), pp. 961-970.

In this study a Value Orientations Scale was developed and administered to Cuban immigrant and Anglo-American adolescents. The Cubans tend to prefer lineality, subjugation to nature, present time, and not to endorse idealized humanistic values, whereas the Anglo-Americans tend to prefer individuality, mastery over nature, future time, and to endorse idealized humanistic values. Clinical implications of the findings are discussed.

0699. Szapocznik, J. et. al. "Comparison of Cuban and Anglo-American Cultural Values in a Clinical Population." Journal of Consulting and Clinical Psychology, Vol. 47, No. 3 (July 1979), pp. 623-624.

This study replicates the previous one, using a adult population in outpatient treatment. Results indicate that the two groups differ in relational, temporal, and person-nature orientations, confirming previous findings.

0700. Taft, Philip B., Jr. "The Cuban Crisis in Miami's Jails." Corrections Magazine, Vol. 8 (April 1982), pp. 35-40.

0701. Thomas, John F. "Cuban Refugees in the United States." International Migration Review, Vol. 1, No. 2 (Spring 1967), pp. 46-57.

This article describes the mandates of the Cuban Refugee Program and documents the services it provided for Cuban refugees.

0702. Center for Advanced International Studies. The Cuban Immigration, 1959-1966, and Its Impact in Miami Dade County, Florida. University of Miami, Coral Gables, 1967.

0703. Walsh, Bryan O. "Cuban Refugee Children." Journal of Inter-American Studies, Vol 13, No. 3-4 (July-October 1971), pp. 378-415.

A chronological account of the efforts by the author and his colleagues to establish the Cuban Children's Program in 1960 and 1961.

0704. Wenk, Michael G. "Adjustment and Assimilation: The Cuban Refugee Experience." International Migration Review, Vol 3, No. 1 (Fall 1968), pp. 38-49.

This survey of 200 Cuban families finds the Cubans to possess the will and energy to become productive and beneficial members of U.S. society. They are self-sufficient, progressive, and grateful. They have a strong desire to adjust and adapt to a new way of life.

0705. Williamson, D. "Adaptation to Socio-Cultural Change: Working-Class Cubans in New Orleans." Caribbean Studies, Vol 16, No. 314 (October 1976/January 1977), pp. 217-227.

This study attempts to test the positive relationship between socio-economic rewards (based on income, occupation, and occupational transferability) and Cuban immigrants' adaptation to socio-cultural change (as measured by degree of socio-cultural integration, degree of psychosomatic stress, and degree of satisfaction with life). Income is found to be the most important factor in the Cubans' adaptation.

0706. Wilson, Kenneth L. and Martin, W. Allen. "Ethnic Enclaves: A Comparison of the Cuban and Black Economies in Miami." American Journal of Sociology, Vol 88, No. 1 (July 1982), pp. 135-160.

This comparison of Cuban and Black businesses in Miami attempts to test hypotheses that link the relative advantage in certain enclaves to the structure of their economies. The results of an input-output analysis suggest that the more advantaged Cuban enclave is characterized by highly interdependent industries, ones which are less dependent on majority industry; while the opposite situation obtains for the less advantaged Black enclave. The paper concludes with a general discussion on the interlinking paths of influence between sociological and economic parameters in the determination of the economic well-being of ethnic enclaves.

0707. Wilson, Kenneth L. and Portes, Alejandro. "Immigrant Enclaves: An Analysis of the Labor Market Experiences of Cubans in Miami." American Journal of Sociology, Vol 86, No. 2 (September 1980), pp. 295-319.

This study of a longitudinal sample of Cuban immigrants confirms the dual labor market hypothesis which defines new immigrants mainly as additions to the secondary labor market linked with small peripheral firms. In addition, the study indicates the existence of an enclave economy associated with immigrant-owned firms. Immigrant workers in this enclave sector share with those in the primary sector a significant economic return to past human capital investment. Such a return is absent among those in the secondary labor market.

0708.  Winsberg, M. D.  "Housing Segregation of a Predominantly Middle Class
Population:  Residential Patterns Developed by the Cuban Immigration into Miami,
1950-1974."  <u>American Journal of Economics and Sociology,</u> VoL  38, No.  4 (October
1979), pp. 403-418.

    Although most Cuban immigrants in Miami have both urban and middle-class
backgrounds, they have come in such large numbers that they are not becoming
residentially assimilated into the non-Latin population.  Cubans and other
Latins have spread throughout the older middle-class residential areas of the
city and replaced other groups who have relocated in such a way that they
are now more separated from each other.

# 5.
# Dominicans in the
# United States

0709. Garrison, V. and Claudewell, C. S. "A Case of a Dominican Migrant." In
Alienation in Contemporary Society: A Multidisciplinary Examination. Eds.,
Bryce-Laporte, R. S. and C. S. Claudewell. New York: Praeger, 1976.

0710. Garrison, Vivian and Weiss, Carol L. "Dominican Family Networks and
United States Immigration Policy: A Case Study." International Migration Review,
VoL 13, No. 2 (Summer 1979), pp. 264-283.

> Analyzes the acculturative process of a Dominican family in New York.
> Argues that the definition of "family" adopted in U.S. Immigration regula-
> tions does not reflect the cooperative kin group in Dominican culture. This
> leads to a variety of extra-legal immigrant adaptive strategies to effect
> reunification of families broken up by immigration policy.

0711. Gonzalez, Nancie S. "Peasant's Progress: Dominicans in New York."
Caribbean Studies, VoL 10, No. 3 (October 1970), pp. 154-171.

> New York City has become the ideal end-point in the rural-to-urban migra-
> tion process of a large number of Dominican peasants. The author describes
> the ways in which this migration process is realized by the peasants, focusing
> on their attempts at obtaining a visa. The article also briefly mentions
> several functions which the migration serves to the Dominican Republic,
> including providing an outlet for excess population, incomes in the form of
> remittances, diffusion of new skills, and employment opportunities for
> Dominicans at home. The author maintains that the migrants tend to main-
> tain their former way of life even though they are living in New York City.

0712. Gonzalez, Nancie S. "Types of Migratory Patterns to a Small Dominican
City and to New York." In Migration and Urbanization: Models and Adaptive
Strategies. Eds., B. M. DuToit and H. I. Safa. The Hague: Mouton, 1975, pp.
209-223.

> This paper examines how migrants' sociocultural lives are molded by their
> background and the configurations of the new environment. It concludes
> that social patterns of Dominican migrants to Santiago (a Dominican city)
> and to New York City tend to resemble those in the country areas from

which they come more than they resemble those of each other after migration
has taken place.  Urbanization per se is not a sufficiently strong socializing
force to create homogeneity.

0713.  Gonzalez, Nancie S.  "Multiple Migratory Experiences of Dominican Women."
Anthropological Quarterly, Vol. 49, No. 1 (January 1976), pp. 36-44.

The majority of lower-class Dominican women migrating to the United States
are engaged in such jobs as domestic service, garment making, and prostitu-
tion.  Regardless of the low social position, a Dominican woman's residence
in the U.S. offers her opportunities not available at home.  The extensive
emigration from the Dominican Republic is related to increasing urban unemployment and the decreasing availability of land in rural areas.

0714.  Hendricks, Glenn.  The Dominican Diaspora:  From the Dominican Republic
to New York City — Villagers in Transition.  New York:  Teachers College Press,
1974.  171 pp.

This study of a group of Dominican peasants who have settled in New York
City describes the social processes triggered by both the process of their
immigration and the resultant resocialization as they adapt to their new
social and cultural environment.  The important variables influencing these
processes include the nature of the cultural experience in the sending society,
the legal and social mechanisms involved in the process of entering the U.S.,
and the socioeconomic niche they have come to occupy in the receiving
society of New York.  This group of Dominican immigrants are described in
the matrix of a larger emergent Spanish subculture in New York.  The author
uses the concept of retribalization to indicate the retention of essential
elements of the world view into which the Dominican immigrant has been
acculturated, while acknowledging that fundamental changes take place in
the content of his/her experiences as a result of immigration and resettlement.

0715.  Hendricks, Glenn L.  "The Phenomenon of Migrant Illegality: The Case of
Dominicans in New York."  In Adaptation of Migrants from the Caribbean in the
European and American Metropolis.  Eds., H. E. Lamur and J. D. Speckmann.
Symposium of the 34th Annual Conference of the American Society for Applied
Anthropology, 1976, pp. 130-142.

Because of their illegal status, the exact number of Dominicans in New York
City is not known.  There is practically no attempt at acculturation, not
even to the larger Hispanic community of New York.  The social network
into which the new arrival is introduced is very close, while the illegal nature
of his/her entry prevents a widening of this network.  Only those who are
completely certain of their legal immigrant status have ventured to move
outside the New York ghetto enclave.

0716.  Hendricks, Glenn L.  "Dominicans."  In Harvard Encyclopedia of American
Ethnic Groups.  Ed., Stephen Thernstrom.  Cambridge: Harvard University Press,
1980, pp. 282-284.

0717.  Kayal, P.  "The Dominicans in New York."  Migration Today, Vol. 6, No. 3
(1978), pp. 16-23; No. 4 (1978), pp. 10-15.

0718.  Lowenthal, David.  "New York's New Hispanic Immigrants."  The Geographical Review, Vol. 66, No. 1 (January 1976), pp. 90-92.

This brief note summarizes some recent writings on New York's Dominican immigrants.

0719. New York Times. "Dominican Immigration to the U.S." May 15, 1970, p. 3.

0720. Pessar, Patricia R. "The Role of Households in International Migration and the Case of U.S.-Bound Migration from the Dominican Republic." International Migration Review, Vol. 16, No. 2 (Summer 1982), pp. 342-364.

This article attempts to demonstrate, with ethnographic data, the importance of households in the migration process. International migration is seen as both an outcome of and an agent for unequal development on a worldwide scale. From an analysis of household strategies, the author argues that Dominican migration occurs as a result of the U.S. economy's demand for a continuous supply of cheap and docile labor, and of the migrant households' need to reproduce themselves at a culturally prescribed level of maintenance.

0721. Sassen-Koob, Saskia. "Formal and Informal Associations: Dominicans and Columbians in New York." Internation Migration Review, Vol. 13, No. 2 (Summer 1979), 314-332.

The incidence and types of voluntary associations in immigrant communities can be seen as an indicator of different modalities of articulation with the receiving society. The relative similarity of cultural-ideological variables in the Columbian and Dominican communities, revealed by the attribution of a common "Hispanic" identity, tends to have less weight in the articulation with the receiving society than the structural differences of their places of origin and the disparity between place of origin and destination. The greater gap and disparity experienced by the Dominicans result in the greater incidence of voluntary associations and their less instrumental character.

0722. Ugalde, Antonio; Bean, Frank D. and Cardenas, Gilbert. "International Migration from the Dominican Republic: Findings from a National Survey." International Migration Review, Vol. 13, No. 2 (Summer 1979), 235-254.

Dominican migrants to the United States are heavily concentrated in the New York/New Jersey region. Using data from a national survey conducted in the Dominican Republic, this study presents the reasons for migration by age, sex, and social strata, as well as the patterns of return migration.

0723. Vicioso, C. "Dominican Migration to the U.S.A." Migration Today, Vol. 20, No. 1 (1976), pp. 59-72.

# 6.
# Puerto Ricans in
# the United States

0724. Abramson, Michael. Palante: The Young Lords Party. New York: McGraw Hill, 1971. 160 pp.

Members of the Young Lords Party, a community organization of Puerto Rican youth in New York, give accounts of their personal lives and their organization.

0725. Ahearn, Frederick L., Jr. "Puerto Ricans and Mental Health: Some Socio-Cultural Considerations." The Urban and Social Change Review, Vol. 12, No. 2 (Summer 1979), pp. 4-9.

This paper offers a historical perspective on Puerto Rican immigration, reviews the association of unemployment and low socioeconomic status with psychological disability, describes some principle values of Puerto Rican culture, and provides suggestions to mental health practitioners.

0726. Alers, J. O. Puerto Ricans and Health Findings from New York City. New York: Hispanic Research Center, Fordham University, 1978. 94 pp.

0727. Attinasi, John. "Language Attitudes in a New York Puerto Rican Community." In Ethnoperspectives in Bilingual Education Research: Bilingual Education and Public Policy in the United States. Ed., R. Padilla. Ypsilanti, MI: Eastern Michigan University, 1979, pp. 408-461.

0728. Baglin, Robert F. "The Mainland Experience in Selected Puerto Rican Literary Works." Ph.D. dissertation, State University of New York at Buffalo, 1971. (DAI: 32/06A, p. 3290)

Examines the experience of Puerto Rican immigrants as reflected in short story, novel, and theater.

0729. Berger, P. "Religion in the Puerto Rican Community of New York City." M.A. thesis, New School for Social Research, 1950.

0730. Berkowitz, Rhoda H. et al. The Impact of Puerto Rican Migration on Governmental Services in New York City. New York: New York University Press, 1957. 74 pp.

0731. Berle, B. Eighty Puerto Rican Families in New York City: Health and Disease Studied in Context. New York: Arno Press, 1975. 331 pp. (Reprint of 1958 edition published by Columbia University Press.)

This is the result of an interdisciplinary study of 80 Puerto Rican households of East Harlem conducted in the early 1950s. Attention is focused on the relationship between social and environmental factors, the susceptibility to illness, and the management of illness. The general susceptibility to illness is high among Puerto Ricans as compared to other segments of the New York City population. Among these families there are marked differences as to the incidence of disease and hospital utilization.

0732. Betances, Samuel. "Puerto Rican Youth." The Rican, Fall 1971, pp. 4-13.

0733. Bettagh, Luz Angeles M. "Family Dynamics in Thirty-Two Puerto Rican Families." Ed. D. dissertation, Columbia University, 1967.

0734. Blatt, Irwin Bruce. "A Study of Culture Change in Modern Puerto Rico: A Comparative Study of the Effect of Social and Economic Change upon Three Puerto Rican Communities which Have Had Varying Degrees of Migration to and from the Mainland." Ph.D. dissertation, New York University, 1973. 246 pp. (DAI: 34/02B, p. 499)

A comparative study of three Puerto Rican villages: one has had little migratory movement to and from the mainland, the second has had significant emigration without return migration, and a third village similar to the second but also having a large return flow. Types of village residents differentiated according to migration experience are compared to ascertain the variations in their incomes, family size, educational aspiration, and other cultural values.

0735. Blaut, James. "Are Puerto Ricans a National Minority?" Monthly Review, Vol. 29, No. 1 (May 1977), pp. 35-55.

The author argues that Puerto Ricans in the mainland U.S. are not merely a national minority, i.e., an ethnic subdivision of the U.S. Rather, these colonial forced migrants constitute a segment of a divided Puerto Rican nation. The point is argued from the Marxist-Leninist perspective on imperialism and colonialism.

0736. Bonilla, Frank and Campos, Ricardo. "A Wealth of Poor: Puerto Ricans in the New Economic Order." Daedalus, Vol. 110, No. 2 (Spring 1981), pp. 133-176.

Puerto Rican migration to the U.S. is the result of a capital-intensive industrialization stategy which has produced unemployment and poverty; it is essentially a process of exchanging people for money. This article describes in detail Puerto Rican immigrants' participation in the U.S. labor force; the inequalities they suffer in terms of education, occupation and income; and the need for them to struggle, along with other minorities, against domestic colonialism in the context of the new economic order.

0737. Bonilla, Frank and Campos, Ricardo. "Imperialist Initiatives and the Puerto Rican Worker: From Foraker to Reagan." Contemporary Marxism, No. 5 (Summer 1982), pp. 1-18.

This article attempts to delineate the circuits and linkages through which capitals, commodities and people have moved between the U.S. and Puerto Rico. This is done through an historical account of the colonial relationship established from the Foraker Act through the New Deal to Reagan's Caribbean Basin Initiative.

0738. Bonilla, Frank and Colon Jordan, Hector. "Puerto Rican Return Migration in the 70s." Migration Today, Vol. 7 (April 1979).

0739. Borrello, Mary Ann and Mathias, Elizabeth. "Botanicas: Puerto Rican Folk Pharmacies." Natural History, Vol. 86, No. 7 (August-September 1977), pp. 65, 67-72.

A photographic essay on the practice of folk medicine and spiritism among New York's Puerto Ricans. The positive effects of the folk religion on individual and communal well-being is highlighted.

0740. Boswell, Thomas D. "Residential Patterns of Puerto Ricans in New York City." The Geographical Review, Vol. 66, No. 1 (January 1979), pp. 92-94.

Summarizes some findings about Puerto Rican immigrants in New York. Unlike earlier immigrants from Europe, they have not dominated the neighborhoods in which they have concentrated. They have continued to reside generally in the poorest areas of the city. At the same time, there has been some degree of segregation within Puerto Rican population itself based on economic differences.

0741. Boykin, Lorraine S. "A Study of the Food and Nutrient Intake of School-Age Puerto Rican Children Living in New York City and Attending a Nutrition Clinic." Ed.D. dissertation, Columbia University, 1970. 148 pp. (DAI: 31/04B, p. 2082)

A study of 90 Puerto Rican children to assess and evaluate the nutrient intake and adequacy of foods consumed by them. With recommendations for implementation by clinic nutritionists.

0742. Brand, Horst. Poverty Area Profiles: The New York Puerto Rican Patterns of Work Experience. New York: U.S. Bureau of Labor Statistics, Middle Atlantic Regional Office, 1971. 62 pp.

Presents data on labor market participation, economic conditions, and social characteristics of Puerto Ricans in Central and East Harlem.

0743. Brown, Myrtle Irene. "Changing Maternity Care Patterns in Migrant Puerto Ricans: A Study of Acculturation in a Group of Puerto Rican Women in New York City, Relevant to the Extent of Their Utilization of Professional Health Care during the Maternity Cycle." Ph.D. dissertation, New York University, 1961. 324 pp. (DAI: 22/12, p. 4330)

This is a case study of 30 Puerto Rican-born women living in New York City. The patterns of their use of professional health services during the maternity cycle are related to: (1) socioeconomic status of the families; (2) primary and secondary group associations; (3) extent of education; and (4) changes in family role behavior and child-rearing beliefs and practices.

0744. Browning, Frank. "From Rumble to Revolution: The Young Lords." Ramparts (October 1970).

Describes the political ideology and community work of the Young Lords of Chicago and New York.

0745. Bucchioni, Eugene. "A Sociological Analysis of the Functioning of Elementary Education for Puerto Rican Children in the New York City Public Schools." Ph.D. dissertation, New School for Social Research, 1965. 243 pp. (DAI: 26/10, p. 6216)

This study is an evaluation of the special programs established for Puerto Rican children by the New York City Board of Education. It indicates that the City's school system has become a middle-class sorting device through which certain children are selected for high academic achievement to insure the continuation of further education and the attainment of middle-class status. In this process Puerto Rican children are sorted out of the channels of successful educational achievement, and are thereby eliminated from access to opportunities based on education.

0746. Campos, Ricardo and Bonilla, Frank. "Bootstraps and Enterprise Zones: The Underside of Late Capitalism in Puerto Rico and the United States." Review, Vol. 5, No. 4 (Spring 1982), pp. 556-590.

This paper examines the current reconcentration and restratification of capitals, markets, and labor power in the capitalist economic system. The implications for Puerto Rico and the U.S. are discussed. This provides a background for the understanding of the movement of people between the two areas.

0747. Campos, Ricardo and Flores, Juan. National Culture and Migration: Perspectives from the Puerto Rican Working Class. New York: Centro de Estudios Puertorriquenos Working Paper, 1978.

0748. Canino, I. A.; Earley, B. F. and Rogler, L. H. The Puerto Rican Child in New York City: Stress and Mental Health. New York: Hispanic Research Center, Fordham University, 1980. 122 pp.

0749. Canino, I. A. and Canino, G. "Impact of Stress on the Puerto Rican Family: Treatment Consideration." American Journal of Orthopsychiatry, Vol. 50, No. 3 (July 1980), pp. 535-541.

This paper describes the impact of migration on the urban, low-income Puerto Rican family in the U.S. Under stress, the Puerto Rican family is subjected to dysfunctional patterns of behavior. The authors suggest the ecostructural family therapy approach as a treatment and mention the many pitfalls that therapists must beware of.

0750. Centro de Estudios Puertorriquenos. "Puerto Ricans in the U.S.: Growth and Differentiation of a Community." In Caribbean Migration to the United States. Eds., R. S. Bryce-Laporte and D. M. Mortimer. Washington, DC: Smithsonian Institution, Research Institute on Ethnic Studies, Occasional Papers No. 1, 1976, pp. 83-110.

0751. Centro de Estudios Puertorriquenos. Documents of the Puerto Rican Migration. New York: Centro de Estudios Puertorriquenos, City University of New York, 1977. 51 pp.

0752. Centro de Estudios Puertorriquenos. Bilingualism and Public Policy: Puerto Rican Perspectives. New York: Centro de Estudios Puertorriquenos, City University of New York, 1979. 88 pp.

0753. Chenault, Lawrence R. The Puerto Rican Migrant in New York City. New York: Columbia University Press, 1938. 190 pp. (Reprint, New York: Russell and Russell, 1970.)

A systematic study of the early Puerto Rican migrants in New York City. The first part of the book discusses the social and economic conditions of Puerto Rico as a source of migration. The second part examines aspects of the immigrants' adaptation on the mainland, including occupation and employment opportunities, housing conditions, the problem of health, and social adjustment.

0754. Cintron, Celia and Vales, Pedro. Return Migration to Puerto Rico. Rio Piedras: Centro de Investigaciones Sociales, Universidad de Puerto Rico, 1974.

0755. Collazo, Francisco. The Education of Puerto Rican Children in the Schools of New York City. San Juan: Department of Education Press, 1954.

0756. Colon, Jesus. A Puerto Rican in New York and Other Sketches. New York: Arno Press, 1975. 202 pp. (Reprint of 1961 edition published by Mainstream Publishers, Inc.)

The author, a journalist and politician, gives some fifty sketches and vignettes of his personal experience in New York City to throw light on "how Puerto Ricans in this city really feel, think, work and live."

0757. Commonwealth of Puerto Rico. Department of Labor, Migration Division. A Summary in Facts and Figures, Progress in Puerto Rico. Puerto Rican Migration. New York, 1956.

Periodic statistical reports on Puerto Rican migration to New York. Published every two years since 1956.

0758. Connors, John T. "A History and Survey of Casita Maria: A Catholic Settlement House in New York City's Spanish Harlem, 1935-1950." M.A. thesis, Fordham University, 1951.

0759. Cooney, S. "Intercity Variations in Puerto Rican Female Participation." Journal of Human Resources, Vol. 14, No. 2 (Spring 1979), pp. 222-235.

This analysis is based on 1970 census data for 56 cities in the mid-Atlantic states. Intercity variations in labor force participation cannot be explained by the socioeconomic characteristics of Puerto Rican female labor supply or assimilation factors. On the other hand, these variations are much more responsive to differences in labor market conditions. The decline of Puerto Rican female participation at the national level is related to the larger numbers of working-age Puerto Rican women still living within the depressed New York labor market.

0760. Cooney, R. S. and Warren, A. E. Colon. "Declining Female Participation Among Puerto Rican New Yorkers: A Comparison with Native White Nonspanish New Yorkers." Ethnicity, Vol. 6, No. 3 (September 1979), pp. 281-297.

Between 1950 and 1970, labor force participation rates of Puerto Rican female workers declined significantly. This study attempts to explain this phenomenon. It finds that changes in the socioeconomic characteristics of Puerto Rican females are not important causal factors. The most significant cause for the decline is educational level. Changes in the demand for female labor by skill levels favor the more educated female groups other than Puerto Ricans.

0761. Cooney, Rosemary S.; Rogler, Lloyd H. and Schroder, Edna. "Puerto Rican Fertility: An Examination of Social Characteristics, Assimilation, and Minority Status Variables." Social Forces, Vol. 59, No. 4 (June 1981), pp. 1094-1113.

This study examines the Goldscheider and Uhlenberg theory of minority group fertility by assessing the importance of assimilation and minority status for Puerto Rican fertility behavior. Findings indicate that assimilation bears almost no relationship to fertility when social characteristics are controlled. On the other hand, minority status insecurity has a direct relationship to lower fertility among younger Puerto Rican women.

0762. Cooney, Rosemary Santana et al. "Decision Making in Intergenerational Puerto Rican Families." Journal of Marriage and the Family, Vol. 44, No. 3 (August 1982) pp. 621-631.

This study starts from the premise that the relationships between decision making and socioeconomic attributes is mediated by sociocultural norms. It is further hypothesized that first generation Puerto Ricans have modified partriarchal norms, while those of the second generation are transitional egalitarian. A comparison of the two generations with their different degrees of assimilation and dissimilar norms, supports the hypothesis that in the parent generation the husband's socioeconomic attributes are inversely related to his power in decision making, while in the second generation the variables are positively related.

0763. Cooper, Paulette, ed. Growing Up Puerto Rican. New York: Arbor House, 1972. 216 pp.

First-person life history narratives of 17 Puerto Rican youths living in New York City. Most of them were born in Puerto Rico and came to the mainland in their early childhood. The majority are of lower-class origin. They talk about their education, sex, family and community life, and relations to other ethnic groups. Their stories are vivid and straight-forward. There is no analytic commentary by the editor.

0764. Cordasco, F. M. "Puerto Rican Child in the American School." Journal of Human Relations, Vol. 15, No. 4 (Fall 1967), pp. 500-509.

This paper discusses the complex pattern of socioeconomic disadvantage, alienation, rejection, and frustrations encountered by Puerto Rican school children. It also evaluates some of the special educational programs designed to meet the needs of Puerto Rican children.

0765. Cordasco, Francesco and Bucchioni, Eugene, eds. Puerto Rican Children in Mainland Schools. Metuchen, NJ: Scarecrow Press, 1968. 465 pp.

0766. Cordasco, Francesco and Bucchioni, Eugene, eds. Education Programs for Puerto Rican Students: Evaluation and Recommendations. Jersey City: Board of Education, 1971. 45 pp.

0767.  Cordasco, Francesco and Bucchioni, Eugene, eds.  The Puerto Rican Experience:  A Sociological Sourcebook.  Totowa, NJ: Rowman and Littlefield, 1973.  370 pp.

This collected volume is divided into four parts: (1) the island background; (2) the migration; (3) conflict and acculturation among Puerto Rican immigrants; and (4) education for Puerto Rican children.  All selections are reprints, and an annotated bibliography, is included.

0768.  Cordasco, F. M. and Covello, L.  "Studies of Puerto Rican Children in American Schools.  A Preliminary Bibliography."  Journal of Human Relations, Vol. 16, No. 2 (Spring 1968), pp. 264-285.

0769.  Costello, C.  "A Study of a Migrant Puerto Rican Minority in a New York City Parish."  M.A. thesis, Fordham University, 1956.

0770.  Crespo, P. C. de.  "Puerto Rican Women Teachers in New York: Self-Perception and Work Adjustments as Perceived by Themselves and Others."  M.A. thesis, Columbia Teachers College, 1965.

0771.  Delgado, M.  "Puerto Rican Spiritualism and the Social Work Profession." Social Casework, Vol. 58, No. 8 (October 1977), pp. 451-458.

This paper describes the practice of spiritualism among Puerto Ricans and the differences between spiritualism and social work practice.  The social work profession is urged to recognize and utilize the sociocultural concepts underlying spiritualism in treating Puerto Rican clients.

0772.  Dolan, Marie B.  "A Study of the Ecological Problems of Puerto Rican Migration and Resettlement."  M.A. thesis, Fordham University, 1951.

0773.  Donahue, F. M.  "A Study of the Original Puerto Rican Colony in Brooklyn, 1938-1943."  M.A. thesis, Fordham University, 1945.

0774.  Donchian, Daniel.  A Survey of New Haven's Newcomers:  The Puerto Ricans.  New Haven: Human Relations Council of Greater New Haven, 1959.

0775.  Dworkis, M., ed.  The Impact of Puerto Rican Migration on Governmental Services in New York City.  New York: New York University Press, 1957.  74 pp.

Assesses the impact of Puerto Rican migration on programs in education, employment, health care, housing, and welfare.

0776.  Estades, Rosa.  Patterns of Religious Participation of Puerto Ricans in New York City.  Rio Piedras: Editional Universitaria, Universidad de Puerto Rico, 1978.  94 pp.

0777.  Fernandez-Pol, B.  "Culture and Psychopathology: A Study of Puerto Ricans."  American Journal of Psychology, Vol. 137, No. 6 (June 1980), pp. 724-726.

This study of 117 lower-class Puerto Rican psychiatric patients in New York attempts to test the link between acceptance of traditional Latin American family values and the development of psychopathology.  The data indicate that in poorer immigrants psychiatric morbidity is accompanied by evidence of decreased adherence to Latin American family beliefs.

0778. Fishman, J. and Terry, Charles. "The Validity of Census Data on Bilingualism in a Puerto Rican Neighborhood." American Sociological Review, Vol. 34, No. 5 (October 1969), pp. 636-650.

A methodological discussion without presenting substantive data.

0779. Fishman, Joshua A. et al. Bilingualism in the Barrio. Washington, DC: U.S. Department of Health, Education and Welfare, 1968. 1209 pp.

A compendium of studies on bilingualism among the Puerto Ricans of New York City. Three major groups of papers are included: sociologically-oriented, psychologically-oriented and linguistically-oriented studies.

0780. Fitzpatrick, Joseph P. "The Integration of Puerto Ricans." Thought, Vol. 30, No. 118 (Autumn 1955), pp. 402-420.

0781. Fitzpatrick, Joseph P. "Attitudes of Puerto Ricans Toward Color." American Catholic Sociological Review, Vol. 20, No. 3 (Fall 1959), pp. 219-233.

0782. Fitzpatrick, Joseph P. "Crime and Our Puerto Ricans." Catholic Mind, Vol. 58, No. 1197 (January-February 1960), pp. 39-51.

0783. Fitzpatrick, J. P. "The Adjustment of Puerto Ricans to New York City." Journal of Intergroup Relations, Vol. 1, No. 1 (Winter 1959/60), pp. 43-51.

This paper discusses the relation of prejudice and discrimination to the process of adjustment among Puerto Rican immigrants. It is suggested that the cultural adjustment of Puerto Ricans will be easier than that of earlier groups of immigrants.

0784. Fitzpatrick, J. P. "Puerto Ricans in the U.S. and Delinquency." Interracial Review (January 1960), pp. 16-20.

0785. Fitzpatrick, J. P. "Intermarriage of Puerto Ricans in New York City." American Journal of Sociology, Vol. 71, No. 4 (January 1966), pp. 395-406.

This study examines marriages of first- and second- generation Puerto Ricans in the years 1949 and 1959. Findings indicate a significant increase in out-group marriage among second-generation Puerto Ricans in New York. There is also a change to lower age at marriage among second- generation Puerto Ricans. There is a tendency for females to marry out in order to marry up. Marriage ceremonies are increasingly of the types characteristic of the host society. All these trends indicate that the process of assimilation to U.S. culture is accelerating rapidly.

0786. Fitzpatrick, J.P. "The Puerto Rican Family." In Ethnic Families in America: Patterns and Variations. Eds., G.H. Mindel and R.W. Habenstein. New York: Elsevier, 1976.

0787. Fitzpatrick, Joseph. P. "Puerto Ricans in Perspective: The Meaning of Migration to the Mainland." International Migration Review, Vol. 2, No. 2 (Spring 1968), pp. 7-20.

The author argues for an interpretation which brings into consideration both the unique characteristics of the Puerto Rican people and the unique charac-teristics of New York City. In this framework, the Puerto Ricans are seen to face some particular problems in relation to the three basic factors on which the identity of other groups was firmly anchored: nationality, color, and religion. Despite these factors which undermined the development of a strong sense of community and identity, the author observes a new trend among Puerto Ricans in the shift from an emphasis on culture as the basis for community to an emphasis on power. He is optimistic that this effort to promote their political interests will strengthen Puerto Rican identity and community.

0788. Fitzpatrick, Joseph P. Puerto Rican Americans: The Meaning of Migration to the Mainland. Englewood Cliffs: Prentice-Hall, 1971. 192 pp.

This study of Puerto Rican immigrants in New York City is focused on their quest for identity. The difficulties of achieving a strong sense of identity are examined in chapters dealing with the following aspects of Puerto Rican experience: (1) the background of uncertainty on the island; (2) the transitory and fragmentary nature of the New York Puerto Rican community; (3) the weakening of family ties; (4) the split along color lines; (5) the problem of religious differences; and (5) a series of problems in education, welfare, mental illness, and drug abuse.

0789. Fitzpatrick, Joseph P. "Puerto Ricans." In Harvard Encyclopedia of American Ethnic Groups. Ed., Stephen Thernstrom. Cambridge: Harvard University Press, 1980, pp. 858-867.

0790. Fleisher, B. "Some Economic Aspects of Puerto Rican Migration to the United States." Ph.D. disseration, Stanford University, 1961. 209 pp. (DAI: 22/10, p. 3434)

This study analyzes Puerto Rican migration as a response to interregional labor market disequilibrium. The principal independent variables examined are relative income levels, job opportunities, and transportation costs. Also contains a discussion of some aspects of the impact of the migration upon both the source and receiving regions.

0791. Fleisher, Belton M. "Some Economic Aspects of Puerto Rican Migration to the United States." Review of Economics and Statistics, Vol. 45, No. 3 (August 1963), pp. 245-253.

Puerto Rican migration is seen as an adjustment process by means of which supply and demand in labor markets are brought into interregional equilibrium. In this case, migration is more closely associated with labor market conditions in the receiving area than with those in the source area. The unemployment rates in Puerto Rico have practically no influence on net migration.

0792. Flores, Juan; Attinasi, John and Pedraza, Pedro, Jr. "La Carreta Made a U-Turn: Puerto Rican Language and Culture in the United States." Daedalus, Vol. 110, No. 2 (Spring 1981), pp. 193-217.

Through a study of the language practice in New York's El Barrio and an analysis of Tato Laviera's poetry, this essay challenges the assumptions held in orthodox discussion of assimilation and bilingualism. It is argued that the language practice of Puerto Ricans constitutes a dynamic bilingualism; it is neither a malady, nor a merely transitory stage. More generally, the authors argue for a class and historical perspective, as opposed to a racial and ethnic framework, for the study of cultural transformation.

0793. Friedel, F. The Negro and the Puerto Rican in American History. Boston: Heath, 1964.

0794. Furst, Philip W. Puerto Ricans in New York City. New York: Puerto Rican Social Services, 1963. 81 pp.

Presents data on housing, education, health, delinquency, and employment.

0795. Galloway, Lowell E. and Vedder, Richard K. "Location Decisions of Puerto Rican Immigrants to the United States." Social and Economic Studies, Vol. 20, No. 2 (June 1971), pp. 188-197.

This paper uses regression analysis to explain the distribution of Puerto Ricans in the U.S. as of the 1960 Census. They are found to be highly sensitive to interstate income differentials in their location decisions. The number of Puerto Ricans in a state is affected by its distance from New York and Miami. Finally, the number of Puerto Ricans in a state is positively related to the population size of that state. Overall, Puerto Ricans' location decisions are responsive to differential economic advantages.

0796. Garcia Olivero, Carmen. Study of the Initial Involvement in the Social Services by the Puerto Rican Migrants in Philadelphia. New York: Basic Books, 1971. 316 pp.

0797. Garrison, V. "Doctor, Espiritista or Psychiatrist? Health-Seeking Behavior in a Puerto Rican Neighborhood of New York City." Medical Anthropology, Vol. 1, No. 2 (Spring 1977).

0798. Garza, Catarino, ed. Puerto Ricans in the U.S.: The Struggle for Freedom. New York: Pathfinder Press, 1977. 63 pp.

0799. Ghali, S. B. "Culture Sensitivity and the Puerto Rican Client." Social Casework, Vol. 58, No. 8 (October 1977), pp. 459-474.

Migration has produced among Puerto Ricans a condition of marginality which is stressful and often conducive to mental breakdown. The traditional family stability and parental authority are affected by the conditions of life in mainland urban centers. This paper discusses the Puerto Rican's attitude and approach toward mental health services, as well as needed improvements in health care programs for the Puerto Rican client. The paper is followed by a commentary by Emelicia Mizio who presents additional thoughts regarding the need for knowledge of and sensitivity to cultural factors in relation to Puerto Rican clients.

0800. Glazer, Nathan. "New York's Puerto Ricans: Formation and Future of a New Community." Commentary (December 1958).

0801. Glazer, Nathan. "The Puerto Ricans." Commentary, Vol. 36, No. 1 (July 1963), pp. 1-9.

This article is adapted from a chapter of Glazer and Moynihan's Beyond the Melting Pot. In it the author discusses the Puerto Rican community of New York during the 1940s and 1950s. Comparisons are made to New York's Blacks and other ethnic groups.

0802.  Golub, Fred T.  The Puerto Rican Worker in Perth Amboy, New Jersey.
New Brunswick:  Rutgers University, Institute of Management and Labor Relations
Occasional Studies No. 2, 1956.  18 pp.

0803.  Gonzalez, Juan.  "Puerto Ricans on the Mainland."  Perspectives:  The
Civil Rights Quarterly, Vol. 13, No. 3 (Winter 1982), pp. 9-17.

  Puerto Ricans have the highest incidence of poverty of any ethnic group in
  the U.S.  In times of economic recession and budget cutting of the 1980's,
  they will suffer increased discrimination and civil rights violation.

0804.  Gonzalez, Pedro.  "Puerto Rican Migration Office:  History and Function
of the Office of the Government of Puerto Rico in New York City, 1948-1952."
M.A. thesis, Fordham University, 1953.

0805.  Gosnell, P. A.  "The Puerto Ricans in New York City."  Ph.D. dissertation,
New York University, 1945.  206 pp.  (DAI: W1945, p. 53)

0806.  Gosnell, P. A.  The Puerto Ricans in New York City.  New York:  New
York University Press, 1949.

0807.  Gray, Lois S.  "Economic Incentives to Labor Mobility:  The Puerto Rican
Case."  Ph.D. dissertation, Columbia University, 1967.  270 pp.(DAI: 27/08A, p.
2263)

0808.  Gray, Lois S.  "The Jobs Puerto Ricans Held in New York City."  Monthly
Labor Review, Vol. 98 (October 1975), pp. 12-16.

0809.  Haberman, Paul W.  "Psychiatric Symptoms among Puerto Ricans in New
York City."  Ethnicity, Vol. 3, No. 2 (June 1976), pp. 133-144.

  This survey study finds that higher symptom scores are reported by Puerto
  Ricans living in Puerto Rico than by those living in New York City.  This
  difference is related to culturally patterned differences in modes of
  expressing distress.

0810.  Hamell, Pete.  "Coming of Age in Nueva York."  New York, Vol. 2 (November
24, 1969), pp. 33-47.

  A journalistic account of Puerto Rican life in New York City, with emphasis
  on the younger generation.  A growing sense of identification with the city
  is highlighted.

0811.  Handlin, Oscar.  The Newcomers:  Negroes and Puerto Ricans in a Changing
Metropolis.  Cambridge:  Harvard University Press, 1959.  171 pp. (Second edition,
Garden City: Doubleday, 1962).

  An examination of the processes and problems of integration of Blacks and
  Puerto Ricans in New York City.  The focus is on patterns of adjustment and
  forms of social action among the two groups.  Comparisons with other immigrant groups are given.

0812.  Hardy-Fanta, C. and MacMahon-Herrera, E.  "Adapting Family Therapy to
the Hispanic Family."  Social Casework, Vol. 62, No. 3 (March 1981), pp. 138-148.

This is a case study of a Puerto Rican immigrant family. The family's under-organization and the family therapy used to reorganize it are described. The authors used this case history to indicate the importance of an under-standing of Hispanic values and family structure for the mental health clinician.

0813. Hardwood, Alan. Rx: Spiritist as Needed: A Study of a Puerto Rican Community Mental Health Resource. New York: John Wiley & Sons, 1977. 251 pp.

0814. Harwood, Alan. "Mainland Puerto Ricans." In Ethnicity and Medical Care. Ed., Alan Harwood. Cambridge: Harvard University Press, 1981, pp. 397-481.

A review of the chief causes of mortality and morbidity among Puerto Ricans reveals that the major health problems of this ethnic group result from class inequality. The article discusses in length the implications of the Puerto Ricans' cultural conceptions of illness and treatment, their language preferences, their patterns of social interaction, and their expectations of medical care.

0815. Hauberg, Clifford A. Puerto Rico and the Puerto Ricans. New York: Twayne Publishers, The Immigrant Heritage of America Series, 1974. 211 pp.

The first half of this book gives an account of the social and political history of Puerto Rico. The second half is devoted to migration and Puerto Ricans in the U.S. These aspects of immigration are examined in detail: the flow of migration; settlement and dispersion on the mainland; assimilation and acculturation of the immigrants; and immigrant achievement in several professions.

0816. Hemos Trabajado Bien. A Report on the First National Conference of Puerto Ricans, Mexican Americans and Educators on the Special Needs of Puerto Rican Youth. New York: Aspira, 1968.

0817. Hernandez Alverez, J. Return Migration to Puerto Rico. Berkeley: Institute of International Studies, University of California, 1967. 153 pp.

Based on a 25 percent sample of the 1960 census of Puerto Rico, this study analyzes the characteristics of migrants and of those who return to the island.

0818. Hernandez Alvarez, J. "The Movement and Settlement of Puerto Rican Migrants within the United States, 1950-1960." International Migration Review, Vol. 2, No. 2 (Spring 1968), pp. 40-52.

This article presents a concise summary of the geographic movement and settlement of Puerto Ricans within the U.S. from 1950 to 1960, based on data drawn from the 1960 census. The author observes a shift away from New York City both in terms of migration from the Island and internal movements between the states. The Puerto Rican population within the U.S. was highly mobile, and where local mobility occurred, it was usually in the direction of neighborhoods marked by outmigration of non-Puerto Ricans. Settlement patterns in and outside New York City are comapred, and the future trend of dispersion of the second-generation Puerto Rican is predicted.

0819. Hidalgo, Hilda. The Puerto Ricans of Newark, New Jersey. Newark: Aspira, 1971.

0820. History Task Force, Centro de Estudios Puertorriquenos. Labor Migration Under Capitalism: The Puerto Rican Experience. New York: Monthly Review Press, 1979. 287 pp.

A collective research effort examining Puerto Rican migration to the U.S. in the theoretical framework provided by Marx. Population and labor force movements are seen as essential components in the organization of production. Puerto Rican migration is presented as an historical instance of a global movement that has been a part of world capitalist development for almost two centuries. The historical section of the book examines Puerto Rican migration in the context of colonialism, agrarian capitalism, and industrialization from the 1870's to the present. Also contains three chapters by individual authors which are listed and annotated separately.

0821. Hogle, Janice; Pelto, Pertti J. and Schensul, Stephen L. "Ethnicity and Health: Puerto Ricans and Blacks in Hartford, Connecticut." Medical Anthropology, Vol. 6, No. 3 (Summer 1982), pp. 127-146.

0822. Horwitz, Julius. The Inhabitants. New York: New American Library, 1960. 174 pp.

0823. Hunker, H. "The Problem of Puerto Rican Migrations to the U.S." Ohio Journal of Science, Vol. 51 (November 1951), pp. 342-346.

0824. International Migration Review. "The Puerto Rican Experience on the U.S. Mainland." Vol. 2, No. 2 (Spring 1968), pp. 7-102. (A special issue)

0825. Jackson, L. P. "Culture or Color? The Moyetos of San Juan and New York." The Crisis, Vol. 75 (July 1968) pp. 189-193.

0826. Jaffe, Abram J., ed. Puerto Rican Population of New York City. New York: Arno Press 1975. 61 pp. (Reprint of 1954 edition published by the Bureau of Applied Social Research, Columbia University.)

Contains three chapters: (1) an analysis of demographic and labor force characteristics of the New York Puerto Rican population; (2) the vital statistics of this population; (3) its social and welfare statistics.

0827. Jenkins, Shirley. Intergroup Empathy: An Exploratory Study of Negro and Puerto Rican Groups in New York City. Ann Arbor: University Microfilms, 1958.

0828. Jennings, James. Puerto Rican Politics in New York City. Washington, DC: University Press of America, 1977. 275 pp.

This study differentiates and analyzes three major types of political leader in the Puerto Rican community of New York City: the electoral politician, the bureaucrat-politician, and the "poverty-crat" politician. The origins of and relationships between these leadership patterns are examined. The political development of the Puerto Rican community is compared to those of earlier European immigrants and Blacks. The author also considers the effects the Puerto Rican politicians will have on New York City politics.

0829. Kantrowitz, Nathan. "Social Mobility of Puerto Ricans: Education, Occupation, and Income Changes Among Children of Migrants, New York, 1950-1960." International Migration Review, Vol. 2, No. 2 (Spring 1968), pp. 53-72.

This paper analyzes the Census statistics of 1950 and 1960 for New York concerning Puerto Ricans. Results show that in New York between 1950 and 1960 the children of Puerto Rican immigrants were upwardly mobile: they attained some high school education, certain white collar jobs, and to a lesser extent, higher income. First-generation immigrants are still poor, and so are their children compared to the national average. The author concludes by predicting that the Puerto Ricans would very probably achieve a social class distribution similar to that of other groups in New York City.

0830.  Kantrowitz, Nathan.  Negro and Puerto Rican Population of New York City in the 20th Century.  New York: American Geographical Society, Studies in Urban Geography No. 1, 1969. 4 pp.

0831.  Kelly, Lenore M.  "Community Identification Among Second Generation Puerto Ricans: Its Relation to Occupational Success."  Ph.D. dissertation, Fordham University, 1965.  357 pp.  (DAI: 32/04A, p. 2223)

This is a study of second generation Puerto Ricans living in Brooklyn. It is found that occupational success does not necessitate a break with one's ethnic community. The occupationally successful Puerto Ricans are more likely to retain a close relationship with their ethnic community, to express a pride in their ethnic identity, and to seek to perpetuate it in their children. On the other hand, the loss of community strength and ethnic identity, and the weakening of ties with one's cultural past are more likely to be associated with occupational failure.

0832.  King, Lourdes Miranda.  "Puertorriquenas in the United States: The Impact of Double Discrimination."  Civil Rights Digest, Vol. 6 (Spring 1974), pp. 20-27.

The Puerto Rican woman in the U.S. feels the impact of a special discrimination as a woman, a Black, and as a Puerto Rican.

0833.  Koss, Joan D.  "Puerto Ricans in Phildelphia: Migration and Accommodation."  Ph.D. dissertation, University of Pennsylvania, 1976.  539 pp.  (DAI: 26/09, p. 4958)

This ethnographic study examines cultural change and reorganization among Puerto Rican immigrants as well as the effects of their prior experiences. Focal aspects of Puerto Rican life in Philadelphia are described: family structure and kinship organization; patterns of friendship and neighboring; and the development and function of voluntary associations. The author emphasizes that post-migration events in Philadelphia, for both the individual and the group, are patterned by a repetitive sequence of phases, a process of rearrangements and adaptive changes.

0834.  Kreidler, Charles W.  A Study of the Influence of English on the Spanish of Puerto Ricans in New Jersey City, New Jersey.  Ann Arbor: University Microfilms, 1958.

0835.  Kurtis, Arlene H.  Puerto Ricans, From Island to Mainland.  New York: J. Messner, 1969.

0836.  Language Policy Task Force.  "Language Policy and the Puerto Rican Community."  The Bilingual Review, Vol. 5, No. 1-2 (January-August 1978), pp. 1-40.

0837. Language Policy Task Force. Social Dimensions of Language Use in East Harlem. New York: Centro de Estudios Puertorriquenos, Working Papers No. 7, 1980. 79 pp.

This sociolinguistic study shows that among the Puerto Ricans of East Harlem the issue of language use is not a dichotomy: either Spanish or English. Rather both languages occur in many ranges of usage. Spanish is desired or considered important by the majority, though not seen as essential to the community identity. English also is desired, and Puerto Rican culture is seen as compatible with English. A large part of the paper is devoted to quantitative analyses of language use in a bilingual setting, especially the phenomenon of code-switching.

0838. Larsen, Ronald J. The Puerto Ricans in America. Minneapolis: Lerner Publications, 1973. 87 pp.

0839. LaRuffa, Anthony L. "Pentecostalism and Assimilation: Puerto Rico and New York City." Journal of the Steward Anthropological Society, Vol. 1, No. 2 (Spring 1970), pp. 113-120.

0840. Leavitt, Ruby R. The Puerto Ricans: Culture Change and Language Deviance. Viking Fund Publications in Anthropology No. 51. Tucson: University of Arizona Press, 1974. 268 pp.

This study investigates the validity of the theory that stuttering is a deviant linguistic response to sociocultural stress. Puerto Rican migrants living in San Juan and New York are compared to ascertain the causal relationship between adaptation and stuttering. This monograph provides detailed accounts of sociocultural adaptation and economic adjustment of the migrants in San Juan and New York.

0841. Leibowitz, M. "Felt-Prejudice and Alienation of the Puerto Rican Migrants in New York City." M.A. thesis, Columbia University, 1955.

0842. Lennon, John. "A Comparative Study of the Patterns of Acculturation of Selected Puerto Rican Protestant and Roman Catholic Families in an Urban Metropolitan Area (Chicago)." Ph.D. dissertation, University of Notre Dame, 1963. 249 pp. (DAI: 24/06, p. 2613)

This study is based on interviews with 50 Protestant and 50 Catholic Puerto Rican couples of lower socio-economic class in Chicago. These Puerto Ricans have generally low acculturation scores. Age and religiosity are found to be significantly related to acculturation. However, there is no significant relationship between acculturation and the following: rural or urban origin, sex, religion, and length of residence in the U.S. of the immigrant.

0843. Levine, Barry B. Benjy Lopez: A Picaresque Tale of Emigration and Return. New York: Basic Books, 1980. 202 pp.

This work is a sociological as well as literary account of the life of a Puerto Rican immigrant. The author first sets up a theoretical and methodological framework in the Introduction. The core of the book is devoted to the protagonist's story, "a picaresque adventure in which the hero works his way through and around the labyrinth of race, ethnicity, class, and bureaucracy in the cosmopolitan world of New York City." The story follows the hero's return to Puerto Rico after a 20-year stay in New York. In the final part of the book the author attempts to locate the phenomenon of Puerto Rican emigration within the context of an imperial development.

0844. Lewis, Oscar. La Vida: A Puerto Rican Family in the Culture of Poverty; San Juan and New York. New York: Random House, 1966. 699 pp.

The classic and controversial study of the life history of a poor family in San Juan and New York. Lengthy autobiographic accounts by members of the extended family are presented. The material is used by the author to test the concept of the culture of poverty.

0845. Lewis, Oscar. A Study of Slum Culture: Background for La Vida. New York: Random House, 1968. 240 pp.

Detailed case studies of 100 poor households in the slums of San Juan and their relatives living in New York City. The author examines the problems of adjustment and changes in the family life of migrants to New York.

0846. Lockett, Edward B. The Puerto Rican Problem. New York: Exposition Press, 1964. 196 pp.

0847. Lucas, Isidro. Puerto Rican Drop-Outs in Chicago: Numbers and Motivations. Washington, DC: U.S. Office of Education, Bureau of Research, 1971. 100 pp.

0848. Lugo-Pagan de Slosser, Hada I. "The Symbolism of Food Among New York Puerto Ricans: A Cultural Account." Ed.D. dissertation, Columbia University Teachers College, 1977. 486 pp. (DAI: 39/12B, p. 5864)

This study views food habits as an integral entity within the household and total family life styles. Food related activities among Puerto Rican New Yorkers are seen as a means to maintain solidarity of the family and community.

0849. MacDonald, Kathleen J. "Child Placement Requests from Puerto Rican Families." M.A. thesis, Fordham University, 1951.

0850. Macisco, John J., Jr. "Assimilation of the Puerto Ricans on the Mainland: A Socio-Demographic Approach." International Migration Review, Vol. 2, No. 2 (Spring 1968), pp. 21-39.

This paper reviews breifly the use of the term assimilation by sociologists and suggests that the analysis of socio-demographic variables is useful to the study of assimilation. The author uses 1960 census data to compare first- and second-generation Puerto Ricans. He finds that second-generation Puerto Ricans have a higher level of schooling, are less likely to be unemployed, have higher incomes, are employed in higher status occupations, marry earlier, tend to marry non-Puerto Ricans in greater proportion, and have fewer children than first-generation Puerto Ricans. These changes in average measures are in the direction of total U.S. averages.

0851. Maldonado, Edwin. "Contract Labor and the Origins of Puerto Rican Communities in the United States." International Migration Review, Vol. 13, No. 1 (Spring 1979), pp. 103-121.

This paper analyses the history of the Puerto Rican movement to the mainland United States as a contract labor group prior to, during and following

World War II. The author shows that the communities which developed from
the early contract labor movement provided the nuclei for present Puerto
Rican communities outside New York.

0852. Maldonado, Rita M. "Why Puerto Ricans Migrated to the United States in
1947-73." Monthly Labor Review, Vol. 99, No. 9 (September 1976), pp. 7-18.

This study indicates that income and unemployment are the primary explanatory
variables of migration flows between Puerto Rico and the United States. However,
the author notes that noneconomic reasons may have become more important
since 1967.

0853. Maldonado-Denis, Manuel. "Puerto Ricans: Protest or Submission." Annals
of the American Academy of Political and Social Science, Vol. 382 (March 1969),
pp. 26-31.

Puerto Rico is seen as a U.S. colony. Its population, both in the island and
on the mainland, is characterized by a pervasive "colonialist syndrome": the
attitude of submission and acquiescence. The author advocates protest and
independence, and sees "Puerto Rican Power" as a complement to Black
Power.

0854. Maldonado-Denis, Manuel. The Emigration Dialectic: Puerto Rico and
the U.S.A. New York: International Publishers, 1980. 156 pp.

In this Marxist study, Puerto Rican emigration is seen as entailed by the
capitalist-colonial mode of production. The strategy of Puerto Rican economic
development is in fact anti-development and anti-nationalistic, the bankruptcy
of which has precipitated the massive exodus of Puerto Ricans from the
island. The author refutes the argument that Puerto Rican emigration is a
voluntary movement of surplus population from the island. The book also
discusses the emigrant's defenselessness in the face of cultural hegemony of
the host society and the problems encountered by Puerto Ricans who have
returned to the island.

0855. Maldonado-Denis, Manuel. "Puerto Rican Emigration: Proposal for Its
Study." Contemporary Marxism, No. 5 (Summer 1982), pp. 19-26.

The author argues that Puerto Rican emigration must be integrated into its
sociohistorical context. Economic factors are the decisive, though not the
only, determinants of migratory process. After a historical sketch, he proposes a periodization of Puerto Rican emigration with suggestions on research
possibilities and strategies.

0856. Malzberg, B. "Mental Disease Among Puerto Ricans in New York City,
1949-1951." Journal of Nervous and Mental Disease, Vol. 23 (March 1956), pp.
262-269.

0857. Mapp, E., ed. Puerto Rican Perspectives. Methuan, NJ: Scarecrow Press,
1974. 171 pp.

0858. Margolis, Richard J. The Losers: A Report on Puerto Ricans and the
Public Schools. New York: Aspira, 1968.

0859. Martinez, Antonio J. "An Analysis of the Present Status of the Teaching
of English as a Second Language to Puerto Rican Adults in New York City." M.A.
thesis, New York Univesity, 1970.

0860.  Martinez, Robert A.  "Dual Ethnicity:  Puerto Rican College Students in New York."  Urban Education, Vol. 14 (July 1979), pp. 254-259.

0861.  Massimine, E. Virginia.  Challenges of a Changing Population: A Study of the Integration of the Puerto Ricans in a West Side Community in Manhattan. New York: Center for Human Relations, New York University, 1954. 35 pp.

0862.  Mayans, Frank, Jr.  "Puerto Rican Migrant Pupils in New York City Schools: A Comparison of the Effects of Two Methods of Instructional Grouping on English Mastery and Attitudes."  M.A. thesis, Columbia Teachers College, 1953.

0863.  Mencher, Joan P.  "Child Rearing and Family Organization Among Puerto Ricans in Eastville:  El Barrio de Nueva York."  Ph.D. dissertation, Columbia University, 1958.  380 pp.  (DAI: 19/05, p. 931)

This ethnographic study focuses on the first generation Puerto Rican immigrants in a slum neighborhood of New York City. It includes a description of child rearing among Eastville Puerto Ricans. Comparisons are made of child training and behavior between extended and nuclear families in the slum and those of Puerto Ricans in rural areas of Puerto Rico. Finally, it is found that members of the Eastville Puerto Rican extended families are the most accepting of change in child rearing behavior and attitudes. In contrast, members of nuclear families tend to accentuate traditional patterns of child rearing practice.

0864.  Metauten, Raymond.  Puerto Ricans in Philadelphia.  Philadelphia:  Commission on Human Relations, 1959.

0865.  Mills, C. Wright; Senior, Clarence and Goldsen, Rose K.  Puerto Rican Journey:  New York's Newest Migrants.  New York: Harper, 1950.  238 pp.  (Reprint, New York: Russell and Russell, 1967.)

Field study of Puerto Ricans in New York City conducted by a Columbia University research team in 1948. It covers conditions in the island, motives for migration, and experience in New York.

0866.  Mintz, Sidney W.  "Puerto Rican Emigration:  A Threefold Comparison." Social and Economic Studies, Vol. 4, No. 4 (December 1955), pp. 311-325.

Based on published works, this paper compares Puerto Rican immigrants in three areas: New York City, St. Croix, and Hawaii. The Hawaiian group are found to be the least successful in social and economic adjustment. The three cases are compared with particular reference to the migration setting, the characteristics of the host society, and those of the migrants themselves.

0867.  Mizio, Emelicia.  Puerto Rican Task Force Report:  Project on Ethnicity. New York:  Family Service Association of America, 1978.  51 pp.

0868.  Monserrat, J.  "School Integration:  A Puerto Rican View."  Integrated Education, Vol. 1 (October/November 1963), pp. 7-12.

0869.  Monserrat, J.  "Puerto Rican Migration: The Impact on Future Relations." Harvard Law Journal, Vol. 15 (Fall 1968), pp. 11-27.

0870.  Montalvo, M.  "The Puerto Rican Migrants of New York City:  A Study of Anomie."  M.A. thesis, Columbia University, 1951.

0871. Morse, Dean W., ed. Pride Against Prejudice: Work in the Lives of Older Blacks and Young Puerto Ricans. Montclair, NJ: Allanheld, Osmun, 1980. 238 pp.

0872. Muldowney, J. "A Study of Catholic Religious Practices of Puerto Rican Migrants in the U.S." M.A. thesis, Fordham University, 1956.

0873. Myers, George C. "Migration and Modernization: The Case of Puerto Rico, 1950-60." Social and Economic Studies, Vol. 16, No. 4 (December 1967), pp. 425-431.

 This paper discusses the role of migration in the process of modernization and regional development of Puerto Rico. External migration resulted in the curtailment of substantial population growth and the attenuation of the trend toward increased urbanization. Nearly all of the island's municipals had experienced net migration losses. Internal migration, compared to emigration, was assuming greater importance.

0874. Myers, George C. and Masnick, George. "The Migration Experience of New York Puerto Ricans: A Perspective on Return." International Migration Review, Vol. 2, No. 2 (Spring 1968), pp. 80-90.

 In this sample of New York Puerto Ricans, one third feel that they will definitely return to the island. The author conducts a comparison between these prospective return movers and stayers. The significant factors which differentiate the prospective returnees are: they tend to see the living conditions and recent development in Puerto Rico more favorably; they tend to maintain closer family ties with the island; they have visited the island more often; and they have lived a somewhat shorter time in their present residences in New York.

0875. National Puerto Rican Task Force on Educational Policy. Toward a Language Policy for Puerto Ricans in the United States: An Agenda for a Community in Movement. New York: Centro de Estudios Puertorriquenos, 1977. 68 pp.

0876. Navarro Hernandez, Pablo. "The Structure of Puerto Rican Families in a Context of Migration and Poverty: An Ethnographic Description of a Number of Residents in El Barrio, New York City." Ed.D. dissertation, Columbia University Teachers College, 1978. 239 pp. (DAI: 39/05A, p. 3016)

 This study focuses on sex and family roles, and attempts to show a logical and coherent structure that enables families to function in the community. Three basic principles are found to underly all kinship relationships in the Puerto Rican community of El Barrio: (1) collaboration of the "hogares"; (2) reciprocity; and (3) matricentrality.

0877. New York City, Board of Education. The Future is Now: The Puerto Rican Study; The Education and Adjustment of Puerto Ricans in New York City. New York, 1958.

0878. New York City, Board of Education. Puerto Rican Study 1953-1957. A Report on the Education and Adjustment of Puerto Rican Pupils in the Public Schools of the City of New York. New York, 1958. 265 pp. (Reprint, New York: Oride Editions, 1972.)

0879. New York City, Department of City Planning. Puerto Rican Migration to New York City. New York, 1957.

0880. New York City, Welfare Council. Puerto Ricans in New York City: The Report of the Committee on Puerto Ricans in New York City of the Welfare Council of New York City. New York: Arno Press, 1975. (Reprint of 1948 edition.)

0881. New York City, Welfare Council. Committee on Puerto Ricans in New York City. The Report of the Committee: Puerto Ricans in New York City. New York, 1948. 60 pp.

0882. New York State, Commission for Human Rights. Puerto Rican Employment in New York City Hotels. A Report by the New York State Commission Against Discrimination, 1958.

0883. New York State, Commission for Human Rights. Puerto Ricans in New York State, 1960-1969. New York, 1969.

0884. New York State Department of Labor. "Puerto Ricans in the New York State Labor Market." Industrial Bulletin, Vol. 36 (August 1957), pp. 17-19.

0885. Novack, Robert T. "Distribution of Puerto Ricans on Manhattan Island." Geographic Review, Vol. 46, No. 2 (April 1956), pp. 182-186.

> Presents the situation as of 1950. Puerto Ricans tended to concentrate in several clusters. Two reasons for this are suggested: (1) low cost housing; (2) nearness to mass transit lines.

0886. O'Brien, Sister Mary Gratia O.P. "Relationship of Self-Perceptions of Puerto Rican and Non-Puerto Rican Parochial School Children to Selected Related Variables." M.A. thesis, Fordham University, 1970.

0887. O'Brien, R.W. "Hawaii's Puerto Ricans: Stereotype and Reality." Social Process in Hawaii, Vol. 23 (1959).

0888. O'Dea, Thomas F. and Poblete, Renato. "Anomie and the Quest for Community: The Development of Sects Among the Puerto Ricans in New York City." American Catholic Sociological Review, Vol. 21, No. 1 (Spring 1960), pp. 18-36.

> A study of the activities of Puerto Rican Pentecostal sects in New York. The religious groups provide a sense of community for the new immigrants.

0889. Padilla, Elena. Suggestions for the Analysis of Family Stresses Among Eastville Puerto Ricans. New York: The Research Institute for the Study of Man, 1956.

0890. Padilla, Elena. Up from Puerto Rico. New York: Columbia University Press, 1958. 317 pp.

> A cultural anthropological study of Puerto Ricans in a poor neighborhood of Manhattan. This book examines the social adaptation of immigrant families to American slum life, focusing on problems of group identity, family relations, child rearing, health, and delinquency.

0891. Pedraja y Santos, Margarita. "The Puerto Rican Newcomer in East Harlem." M.A. thesis, Fordham University, 1953.

0892. Piore, Michael J. "The Role of Immigration in Industrial Growth: A Case Study of the Origins and Character of Puerto Rican Migration to Boston." MIT Department of Economics, Working Paper No. 112, 1973.

0893. Puerto Rican Forum. A Study of Poverty Conditions in New York Puerto Rican Community. New York, 1964. 3rd ed., 1970. 86 pp.

0894. Puerto Rican Forum. The Puerto Rican Community Development Project. New York: Arno Press, 1975. 145 pp. (Reprint of 1964 edition published by Puerto Rican Forum.)

This is a proposal for developing research on and community projects for the Puerto Rican immigrant population. It also contains a chapter on the statistical profile of the Puerto Rican community in New York City as of the early 1960s.

0895. Puerto Rican Research and Resources Center. Ethnic Differences Affecting the Delivery of Rehabilitation Services. New York, 1971.

0896. Puerto Rican Research and Resources Center. A Study of Determinants of Educational Attainment Among Puerto Rican Youth. New York, 1973.

0897. Puerto Ricans and Educational Opportunity. New York: Arno Press, 1975. 189 pp.

A compilation of materials published in the 1960s and early 1970s.

0898. Rand, Christopher. The Puerto Ricans. New York: Oxford University Press, 1958. 178 pp.

A journalistic account of the Puerto Rican immigrants in New York City. The material was originally published in The New Yorker.

0899. Rindfuss, R. R. "Fertility and Migration: The Case of Puerto Rico." International Migration Review, Vol. 10, No. 2 (1976), pp. 191-204.

0900. Rivera, Felipe. "The Puerto Rican Farmworker: From Exploitation to Unionization." In Labor Migration under Capitalism: The Puerto Rican Experience, History Task Force, Centro de Estudios Puertorriquenos. New York: Monthly Review Press, 1979, pp. 239-264.

0901. Rodriguez, Clara E. The Ethnic Queue in the U.S.: The Case of the Puerto Ricans. San Francisco: R. and E. Research Associates, 1974.

0902. Rodriguez, Clara E. "A Cost-Benefit Analysis of Subjective Factors Affecting Assimilation: Puerto Ricans." Ethnicity, Vol. 2, No. 1 (March 1975), pp. 60-80.

This study of a sample of Puerto Ricans in New York attempts to examine their attitudes toward the desirability, feasibility and costs of attempting to assimilate. Findings suggest that Puerto Ricans perceive the benefits of assimilation as being a question of differential probabilities, and that they are acutely aware of general discrimination against them. They are not strongly aware of the social costs they have to bear in order to assimilate, but they perceive some alternatives to assimilation.

0903. Rodriguez, Clara E. "Economic Factors Affecting Puerto Ricans in New York." In Labor Migration Under Capitalism: The Puerto Rican Experience. History Task Force, Centro de Estudios Puertorriquenos. New York: Monthly Review Press, 1979, pp. 197-221.

The author argues that the role of Puerto Rican immigrants in the U.S. has been to depress wage levels and enlarge the ranks of the growing industrial reserve army in the monopoly stage of capitalist development. This has resulted in high unemployment, skewed occupational distribution, and low income among Puerto Ricans. The author examines the specific factors which account for these phenomena. These include: automation, sectoral decline, blue-collar structural unemployment, racial and ethnic prejudice, restrictive union policies, inadequate educational opportunities, and the restriction on Puerto Ricans in government employment.

0904. Rodriguez, Clara E.; Korrol, V. S. and Alers, J. O. The Puerto Rican Struggle: Essays on Survival in the U.S. New York: Puerto Rican Migration Research Consortium, 1980. 151 pp.

0905. Rogler, Lloyd H. "Growth of an Action Group: The Case of a Puerto Rican Migrant Voluntary Association." International Journal of Comparative Sociology, Vol. 9 (September-December 1968), pp. 223-234.

0906. Rogler, Lloyd H. Migrant in the City: The Life of a Puerto Rican Action Group. New York: Basic Books, 1972. 251 pp.

A study of a Puerto Rican citizens group in New Jersey.

0907. Rogler, Lloyd H. "The Changing Role of a Political Boss in a Puerto Rican Migrant Community." American Sociological Review, Vol. 39, No. 1 (February 1974), pp. 57-67.

Based on a field study of a Puerto Rican migrant community, this paper finds that the Puerto Ricans' incentive to form politically independent organizations arises from the evolution of their ethnic identity. Such politically independent ethnic organizations gradually replace the earlier political boss system as the latter ceases to be able to contain or channel the thrust of assimilation.

0908. Rogler, Lloyd H. "Help Patterns, the Family, and Mental Health: Puerto Ricans in the United States." International Migration Review, Vol. 12, No. 2 (Summer 1978), pp. 248-259.

Reports the tentative conclusion of an on-going research: Puerto Ricans adapt well to the new environment on the mainland because of the supportive, help-giving familial and cultural systems. Only those who are unable to be integrated into the supportive systems are rendered psychologically vulnerable.

0909. Rogler, Lloyd H.; Barreras, O. and Cooney, R.S. "Coping with Distrust in a Study of Intergenerational Puerto Rican Families in New York Cities." Hispanic Journal of Behavioral Sciences, Vol. 3, No. 1 (1981), pp. 1-17.

0910. Rogler, Lloyd H.; Cooney, Rosemary Santana and Ortiz, Vilma. "Intergenerational Change in Ethnic Identity in the Puerto Rican Family." International Migration Review, Vol. 14, No. 2 (Summer 1980), pp. 193-214.

This research focuses upon intergenerational changes in ethnic identity within the family. The analysis is guided by the theoretical postulate that ethnic identity is influenced by receptivity to external influences stemming from the host society and by length of exposure to the new environment. Findings indicate that both education and age at arrival have significant independent effects upon the ethnic identity in the family.

0911. Rosenberg, Terry J.  Residence, Employment, and Mobility of Puerto Ricans in New York City.  Chicago: University of Chicago, Department of Geography, 1974. 230 pp.

0912. Rosenberg, Terry J. and Lake, Robert W.  "Toward a Revised Model of Residential Segregation and Succession: Puerto Ricans in New York, 1960-1970."  American Journal of Sociology, Vol. 81, No. 5 (March 1976), pp.  1142-1150.

Low income levels and housing discrimination have inhibited the assimilation of the Puerto Rican minority.  At the same time, an expanding Black population and encroaching urban renewal have prevented the establishment of Puerto Rican concentrations of sufficient scale to allow the development of indigenous political and economic resources.  Finally, the increased mobility and possibility of return migration tends to deprive the group of its organizational elite.  In these characteristics, the Puerto Ricans do not conform to previous models of immigrant residential pattern.

0913. Rosner, Milton S.  "A Study of Contemporary Patterns of Aspirations and Achievements of the Puerto Ricans of Hell's Kitchen."  Ph.D. dissertation, New York University, 1960.  (DAI: 18/05A, p. 1886)

Examines the sociocultural variations related to aspiration and achievement among 100 Puerto Rican families in Hell's Kitchen, New York City.

0914. Ruiz, Paquita.  Vocational Needs of Puerto Rican Migrants.  Rio Piedras: University of Puerto Rico, Social Science Research Center, 1947.

Study of a sample of 3,024 male Puerto Ricans who migrated to New York City during 1940-1944.

0915. Ruiz Canales, Rose.  "Spanish Speaking Residents of East Harlem:  A Study of 54 Short Term Cases Serviced by Catholic Charities Family Division, 1952."  M.A. thesis, Fordham University, 1953.

0916. San Juan Cafferty, Pastora.  "Puerto Rican Return Migration:  Its Implications for Bilingual Education."  Ethnicity, Vol. 2, No. 1 (March 1975), pp.  52-65.

Since the mid-1960s there has been an increasing trend of return migration among Puerto Ricans.  These return migrants and especially their children are the outcasts of two cultures, alienated from two languages.  To overcome this, the author advocates the establishment of bilingual education programs in communities with a large Puerto Rican population.

0917. San Juan Cafferty, P. and Rivera-Martinez, C.  The Politics of Language: The Dilemma of Bilingual Education for Puerto Ricans.  Boulder: Westview Press, 1981. 119 pp.

Chapters deal with language policy, culture, national identity, bilingual education, and migration.  The book includes case studies and an evaluation of bilingual education policy.

0918. Sanchez Korrol, Virginia.  "On the Other Side of the Oceans:  The Work Experiences of Early Puerto Rican Migrant Women."  Caribbean Review, Vol. 8, No. 1 (January-March 1979).

0919. Sandis, Eva. "Characteristics of Puerto Rican Migrants to and from the United States." International Migration Review, Vol. 4, No. 2 (Spring 1970), pp. 22-43.

Compares the educational, occupational, and income data for three groups: Puerto Rican migrants to the mainland, Island inhabitants, and return migrants. In terms of education, migrants had more median years of schooling than Islanders, but less than return migrants. In terms of occupation, there is a trend of downward mobility with migration to the mainland, but a higher percentage of return migrants are white collar workers. The median income of return migrants is significantly less than that of migrants in the U.S., but it is more than that of Island inhabitants. The article concludes that the impact of migration is a significant loss of highly trained workers for Puerto Rico.

0920. Scott, J.F. and Delgado, M. "Planning Mental Health Programs for Hispanic Communities." Social Casework, Vol. 60, No. 8 (October 1979), pp. 451-456.

This paper analyzes the developmental stages and administrative choices of the Worcester, Massachusetts, Youth Guidance Center which serves the local Puerto Rican community. The authors argue that a successful Hispanic mental health program must reflect the needs of the community as well as an appreciation of its cultural values.

0921. Seda Bonilla, Eduardo. "Education and the Cultural Construction of Reality in the Puerto Rican Community, New York." Multilingual Assessment Project, 1974.

0922. Senior, Clarence O. Puerto Rican Emigration. Rio Piedras:  University of Puerto Rico, Social Science Research Center, 1947. 166 pp.

0923. Senior, Clarence O. "The Puerto Rican in a New Community." Community (October 1953).

0924. Senior, Clarence O. "Patterns of Puerto Rican Dispersion in the Continental United States." Social Problems, Vol. 2, No. 2 (October 1954), pp. 93-99.

Puerto Rican immigrants in the U.S. tend to disperse throughout the country in times of economic prosperity and concentrate in clusters in several metropoles in times of recession. Puerto Rican movement to the continent is discussed in terms of spontaneous vs. organized migration, and primary vs. derived settlement. The differential distribution of Puerto Ricans in terms of color and sex is briefly noted.

0925. Senior, Clarence O. "Puerto Rico's Migration to the Mainland." Monthly Labor Review, Vol. 78 (December 1955), pp. 1354-1358.

Deals with Puerto Rican migration during the period 1946-1954. Two flows of immigrants are differentiated: farm laborers and city migrants. Also briefly discusses the work of the migration programs of the Puerto Rican government.

0926. Senior, Clarence O. Strangers, Then Neighbors:  From Pilgrims to Puerto Ricans. New York: Freedom Books, 1961. 86 pp.

This booklet traces the transition from strangers to neighbors among Puerto Rican immigrants. This transition is manifest in educational attainment,

economic improvement, and social integration as also happened to earlier
European immigrants. The mutual acceptance and adjustment between
immigrants and the host society are emphasized throughout the book.

0927. Senior, C.O. The Puerto Ricans: Strangers, Then Neighbors. Chicago:
Quadrangle Books, 1965. 128 pp.

This is a revised and expanded version of the author's 1961 booklet.

0928. Senior, Clarence O. "The Puerto Ricans in New York: A Progress Note."
International Migration Review, Vol. 2, No. 2 (Spring 1968), pp. 73-79.

The author maintains that to the extent that immigrants are found distributed
throughout the institutions of the host society and share in policy making
decisions, then they have become integrated in the larger society. This
article looks for signs of Puerto Ricans' institutional distribution and finds
encouraging progress in the social, religious, and especially economic and
political fields. The Puerto Ricans' economic and political assimilation is at
least equal to, and in some instances greater than that of earlier immigrant
groups.

0929. Senior, Clarence O. and Watkins, Donald O. "Towards a Balance Sheet of
Puerto Rican Migration." In Status of Puerto Rico: Selected Background Studies
for the United States-Puerto Rico Commission on the Status of Puerto Rico.
Washington, DC: U.S. Government Printing Office, 1966, pp. 743-758. (SuDoc
Number: Y3.Un3/5:2St9)

This article shows that the migration from Puerto Rico to the U.S. has tended
to benefit: (1) the migrants and their families, since they typically move to
places where better opportunities exist; (2) the area in which they come to
live, because commodities and services are produced by the immigrants; and
(3) the area from which they migrate, for emigration solves the problem of
unemployment.

0930. Sexton, Patricia C. Spanish Harlem: An Anatomy of Poverty. New York:
Harper and Row, 1965. 208 pp.

This personal testimony is based on the author's two-year residence in the
Puerto Rican section of East Harlem. The community's poverty and its
consequences are examined with particular reference to the following: housing
problems and development; failure in education; religion and church organizations; power structure and political impotence; community unrest and protest.

0931. Siegel, A. "The Social Adjustments of Puerto Ricans in Philadelphia."
Journal of Social Psychology, Vol. 46 (August 1957), pp. 99-110.

This paper summarizes the findings of a study of Puerto Ricans in Philadelphia
conducted in 1953. Research findings relating to social adjustment are
presented, including language, medical, religious, economic and general
urban adjustment.

0932. Siegel, Arthur; Orlans, Harold and Greer, Loyal. Puerto Ricans in
Philadelphia: A Study of Their Demographic Characteristics, Problems and Attitudes. New York: Arno Press, 1975. 135 pp. (Reprint of 1954 edition published
by the Commission of Human Relations, Philadelphia.)

This study is based on a 1953 survey of 209 Puerto Rican households and 102 of their neighbors living in the central portions of Philadelphia. Numerous statistical tables are included. Demographic characteristics of Puerto Rican immigrants, their occupational status, their social adjustment, and the host society's reaction to them are the subjects examined in detail.

0933. Spiaggia, Martin. Self-Group Devaluation and Prejudice in Minority-Group Boys. Ann Arbor: University of Michigan Press, 1959.

0934. Stockton, William. "Going Home: The Puerto Ricans' New Migration." The New York Times Magazine (November 12, 1978), pp. 20-22, 88-93.

Story of a "Neorican" family who returned to Puerto Rico after living 23 years in New York. The returnees compare their lives in the two places.

0935. Stone, Leroy O. "Net Migration and Sex-Age Composition of Puerto Rico 1950-60." Canadian Review of Sociology and Anthropology, Vol. 2, No. 2 (May 1965), pp. 108-116.

Migration is the principal explanatory factor of the change in the sex-age composition of Puerto Rican population. Given its influence on the age structure of population, migration contributed indirectly to the fall in the crude rate of birth and to the decline in the crude rate of male participation in the labor force.

0936. Stuart, Irving R. "Intergroup Relations and Acceptance of Puerto Ricans and Negroes in an Immigrants' Industry." Journal of Social Psychology, Vol. 56 (1962), pp. 89-96.

0937. Stuart, Irving R. "Minorities vs. Minorities: Cognitive, Affective, and Conative Components of Puerto Rican and Negro Acceptance and Rejection." Journal of Social Psychology, Vol. 59 (February 1963), pp. 93-99.

0938. Torres-Matrullo, Christine. "Acculturation and Psychopathology among Puerto Rican Women in Mainland United States." Ph.D. dissertation, Rutgers University, 1974. 98 pp. (DAI: 35/06B, p. 3041)

Based on interviews and tests, this study investigates relationships between level of acculturation (as determined by length of residence and type of marriage) and the occurrence of psychopathology among Puerto Rican women in mainland U.S. It finds that the more acculturated women have a more positive self-concept and self-evaluation; they also score lower on scales of depression and obsessive-compulsion. It is also found that family and sex-role attitudes do not change significantly with level of acculturation, but rather with level of education. Overall, the incidence of schizophrenia is low in this sample population.

0939. Torres-Matrullo, Christine. "Acculturation and Psychopathology among Puerto Rican Women in Mainland United States." American Journal of Orthopsychiatry, Vol. 46, No. 4 (October 1976), pp. 710-719.

This study of 72 Puerto Rican women in New Jersey explores relationships between the stress of acculturation and the existence of psychopathology. Findings indicate that subjects low in acculturation are more likely to exhibit psychopathology and have problems of self-acceptance and negative personality adjustment. On the other hand, family and sex-role related attitudes are found to remain unchanged with acculturation.

0940. Trenton, P. V. "Are Puerto Ricans Negroes?" Negro Digest, Vol. 10 (July 1961), pp. 96-98.

0941. U.S. Commission on Civil Rights. Puerto Ricans in the Continental United States: An Uncertain Future. Washington, DC, 1976. 157 pp.

0942. U.S. Commission on Civil Rights. Western Regional Office. Puerto Ricans in California: A Staff Report. Washington, DC: Government Printing Office, 1980. 19 pp.

0943. U.S. Department of Labor. "The New York Puerto Ricans: Patterns of Work Experience ." In Puerto Rico and Puerto Ricans: Studies in History and Society. Eds., A. Lopez and James Petras. New York: John Wiley and Sons, 1974.

0944. U.S. Department of Labor. A Socio-Economic Profile of Puerto Rican New Yorkers. New York: Bureau of Labor Statistics, 1975.

0945. U.S. Department of Labor. Bureau of Employment Security. Division of Reports and Analysis. Puerto Rican Farm Workers in Florida: Highlights of a Study. Washington, DC: Government Printing Office, 1955. (SuDoc Number: L7.2:P96/4)

0946. U.S. Women's Bureau. Women of Puerto Rican Origin in the Continental United States. Washington, DC, 1977. 4 pp. (SuDoc Number: L36.102:P96)

0947. Vazquez, Hector I. "Puerto Rican Americans." Journal of Negro Education, Vol. 38, No. 3 (Summer 1969), pp. 247-256.

While Puerto Rican children make up one fourth of the public school pupils in New York City, they have the lowest record of achievement of any iden-tifiable ethnic group. This study summarizes the background of the problem, the school situation, community involvement, and concludes with recommen-dations.

0948. Vazquez, J. M. "Accounting for Ethnicity in the Counseling Relationship: A Study of Puerto Rican College Students." Ethnic Groups, Vol. 1, No. 4 (1977), pp. 297-318.

0949. Vazquez Calzada, Jose L. "Demographic Aspects of Migration." In Labor Migration Under Capitalism: The Puerto Rican Experience. History Task Force, Centro de Estudios Puertorriquenos. New York: Monthly Review Press, 1979, pp. 223-236.

0950. Wagenheim, Karl. A Survey of Puerto Ricans on the U.S. Mainland in the 1970's. New York: Praeger, 1975. 133 pp.

0951. Wagenheim, Karl, ed. The Puerto Ricans: A Documentary History. New York: Praeger, 1973. 332 pp.

0952. Wakefield, Dan. Island in the City: The World of Spanish Harlem. New York: Arno Press, 1975. 278 pp. (Reprint of 1959 edition published by Houghton Mifflin.)

A journalistic account of the Puerto Rican neighborhoods of East Harlem, including discussions on the following: the history of migration; religious beliefs and practice; drug use; teenage gangs; education for children; working conditions; community service.

0953.  Weissman, Julius.  "An Exploratory Study of Communication Patterns of Lower Class Negro and Puerto Rican Mothers and Pre-School Children."  M.A. thesis, Columbia Teachers College, 1966.

0954.  Westfried, Alex H.  Ethnic Leadership in a New England Community:  Three Puerto Rican Families.  Cambridge, MA: Schenkman, 1980.  176 pp.

0955.  Wheeler, Helen.  "Puerto Rican Population of New York, New York." Sociology and Social Research, Vol. 35, No. 2 (November–December 1950), pp. 123–127.

A brief note on the historical background of Puerto Rican emigration and the immigrant's social and economic adaptation in New York City.

0956.  Zell, Steven P.  "A Comparative Study of the Labor Market Characteristics of Return Migrants and Non-migrants in Puerto Rico."  Commonwealth of Puerto Rico, Office of the Governor, Planning Board, 1973.

0957.  Zell, Steven P.  "Analyzing Puerto Rican Migration:  Problems with the Data and the Model."  Monthly Labor Review, Vol. 100 (August 1977), pp. 29–35.

0958.  Zell, Steven P. et al.  Puerto Rican Migrants:  A Socio-Economic Study. San Juan: Bureau of Social Planning, 1972.

# 7.
# Haitians in the United States

0959. Anderson, Jervis. "The Haitians of New York." New Yorker, Vol. 51, No. 6 (March 31, 1975), pp. 50, 52-4, 58-9, 60, 62-75.

A journalistic account of Haitians in New York City, estimating that there may be as many as 300,000 of them. They regard themselves as "the silent minority." This article describes the Haitians' treatment by the Immigration Service, their community organizations, and the class division among themselves. A large part of the article is devoted to activities of Haitian artists.

0960. Bogre, Michelle. "Haitian Refugees." Migration Today, Vol. 7, No. 4 (1979).

0961. Boswell, Thomas D. "The New Haitian Diaspora: Florida's Most Recent Residents." Caribbean Review, Vol. 11, No. 1 (Winter 1982), pp. 18-21.

There are about 40,000 to 45,000 Haitians living in Miami. In contrast to the earlier stream of Haitians that was destined for New York and other northern cities, a large part of South Florida's Haitians appear to be arriving by boat, are illegal entrants, and are members of the poorer classes. Most of them come from the northern part of Haiti. They tend to concentrate in large urban areas, and generally live in wretched conditions. They tend to stick together, seldom associating with Blacks or Hispanic Americans.

0962. Buchanan, Susan Huelsebusch. "Language and Identity: Haitians in New York City." International Migration Review, Vol. 13, No. 2 (Summer 1979), pp. 298-313.

Haitian immigrants in New York City have experienced conflicts over social identity and status. This article contends that Haitians express these conflicts in their controversies over language use. The argument is presented through an analysis of a dispute over the primary language—Creole or French--to be used in the Catholic Mass conducted at a Brooklyn church. The language issue also serves as a vehicle for debate over leadership within the Haitian community and representation within American society.

0963. Buchanan, Susan Huelsebusch. "Haitian Women in New York City." Migration Today, Vol. 7, No. 4 (1979), pp. 19-25, 39.

0964. Buchanan, Susan Huelsebusch. "Scattered Seeds: The Meaning of the Migration for Haitians in New York City." Ph.D. dissertation, New York University, 1980. 524 pp. (DAI: 41/12A, p. 5156)

This study emphasizes cultural factors and the emic viewpoint in the Haitian immigrants' contruction of their lives and social reality. Through a focus on the conflict over language use, this dissertation examines the following aspects of the meaning of migration: (1) the cultural categories of class and color which Haitians bring to the new milieu; (2) public ideologies of the migration as expressed through political organization and the cultural pattern of fragmentation in collective behavior; (3) Haitian migrants' position in and interpretation of the racial, ethnic, legal, and economic structures of incorporation in American society; (4) collective behavior and collective identity in relation to the host society.

0965. Buchanan, Susan Huelsebusch. "Profile of a Haitian Migrant Women." In Female Immigrants to the United States. Eds., D.M. Mortimer and R.S. Bryce-Laporte. Washington, DC: Smithsonian Institution, Research Institute for Ethnic Studies, Occasional Papers No. 2, 1981, pp. 112-142.

Presents a composite profile of a female Haitian immigrant in New York, focusing on her problems and adaptive strategies in employment and sex-role behavior. The article concludes that the migration and resettlement in New York has simultaneously improved and worsened the lives of Haitian women. The significant and independent role of women in migration and resettlement processes are emphasized.

0966. Clerisme, Renald. "Dependency and Migration, A Case Study: Bassin-Bleuans in Brooklyn." M.A. thesis, New York University, 1975.

0967. Colbert, L. "Haitian Aliens - A People in Limbo." The Crisis, Vol. 87, No. 7 (August/September 1980), pp. 235-238.

Argues that the Haitian refugees are really fleeing from political persecution; they are not merely economic refugees. This article also describes the work of the supporters of Haitian political asylum.

0968. Douge, Daniel. Caribbean Pilgrims: The Plight of the Haitian Refugees. Smithtown, NY: Exposition Press, 1982. 87 pp.

0969. Fontaine, P. M. "Haitian Immigrants in Boston: A Commentary." In Caribbean Migration to the United States. Eds., R.S. Bryce-Laporte and D.M. Mortimer. Washington, DC: Smithsonian Institution, Research Institute for Ethnic Studies, Occasional papers No. 1, 1976, pp. 111-129.

0970. Gaines-Carter, Patrice. "Boat People Come Ashore." Black Enterprise, Vol. 10, No. 4 (November 1979), pp. 21-22.

A short note on Haitian businesses in a northwest Miami neighborhood.

0971. Galatioto, Rocco and Buchanan, Susan H. "Haitians in the Arts." Migration Today, Vol. 7, No. 4 (1979).

0972. Glick, Nina. "The Formation of a Haitian Ethnic Group." Ph.D. dissertation, Columbia University, 1975. 338 pp. (DAI: 36/05A, p. 2940)

This dissertation begins with the premise that ethnic identity is not a primitive instinct but a situational response. It then describes efforts made during the years 1969 and 1970 to link members of New York Haitian population into a network of ethnic organizations. The author focuses on the analysis of events in which the immigrants formed relationships with members of various institutions of the host society. The study concludes that even with the support of these institutions the efforts to form a Haitian ethnic group were not successful. In fact, the ideology of American institutions did not support the formation of independent ethnic groups with strong leadership, although it might encourage ethnic group identities and the perception of America as a pluralistic society.

0973. "The Invisible Invasion." Black Enterprise, Vol. 10, No. 9 (April 1980), pp. 29-30.

Argues that since the U.S. cannot absorb all those who would like to come here, the public has to debate on "which tired, which wretched, which poor should be given a chance to become good Americans."

0974. Laguerre, Michel S. "The Impact of Migration on Haitian Family and Household Organization." In Family and Kinship in Middle America and the Caribbean. Eds., Rene Romer and Arnaud Marks. Leiden: Royal Institute of Linguistics and Anthropology, 1978, pp. 446-481.

0975. Laguerre, Michel S. Migration et Vie Rurale en Haiti. Port-au-Prince: InterAmerican Institute of Agricultural Sciences of the Organization of American States and InterAmerican Bank of Development, 1978.

0976. Laguerre, Michel S. Dependence and Ethnicity: The Haitian Community in New York City. New York: Institute for Urban and Minority Education, Teachers College, 1978.

0977. Laguerre, Michel S. "Ticouloute and His Kinfold: The Study of a Haitian Extended Family." In The Extended Family in Black Societies. Eds., D.B. Shimkin; E.M. Shimkin and D.A. Frate. The Hague: Mouton, 1978, pp. 407-445.

After a critical review of studies of Haitian kinship, this article presents a detailed history of an extended family consisting of ten households. These households were located in rural and urban Haiti, and in the U.S. The author concludes that, despite the many factors, including international migration, which have affected the development and functioning of the Haitian extended family, it has remained a functioning, integrated, and situationally adaptive institution.

0978. Laguerre, Michel S. "The Haitian Niche in New York." Migration Today, Vol. 7, No. 4 ( 1979), pp. 12-18.

0979. Laguerre, Michel S. "Haitian in the U.S." In Harvard Encyclopedia of American Ethnic Groups. Ed., Stephen Thernstrom. Cambridge: Harvard University Press, 1980, pp. 446-449.

0980. Laguerre, Michel. "Haitian Americans." In Ethnicity and Medical Care. Ed., Alan Harwood. Cambridge: Harvard University Press, 1981, pp. 172-210.

The data for this paper were gathered mainly in New York City and supplemented with information from Haitians in the San Francisco Bay area. The

author first gives a sketch of the epidemiological characteristics of the
Haitians. Haitian concepts of disease and illness are then discussed in detail.
Their difficulties with mainstream medical system, and alternative sources
of health care, including home treatment and Voodoo medicine, are described.
The paper concludes with some concrete recommendations for health-care
professionals.

0981. Laguerre, Michel S. "Haitian Immigrants in the U.S.: A Historical Overview." In White Collar Migrant Labor in the Americas and the Caribbean. Eds.,
Arnaud Marks et al. Leiden: Royal Institute of Linguistics and Anthropology,
1982.

0982. Laguerre, Michel S. American Odyssey: Haitians in the United States.
Ithaca: Cornell University Press, 1984.

0983. Laguerre, Michel S. "Haitians in the Southern States." In Encyclopedia of
Southern Culture. Eds., William Ferris and Charles Wilson. Chapel Hill:
University of North Carolina Press, forthcoming.

0984. Lampley, J. "Uncharted Future for Haitian Boat People." Africa, No. 17
(May 1981), pp. 60-61.

0985. Laraque, Frank. "Haitian Emigration to New York." Migration Today,
Vol. 7, No. 4 (1979).

0986. Leak, Martha W. "New York's Haitians: Working, Waiting, Watching Bebe
Doc." The New York Times Magazine (October 10, 1971).

0987. Poux, Paddy. "Haitian's Assimilation in the Life and the Future of the
City of New York." M.A. thesis, Fordham University, 1972.

0988. Rey, Kitty Hyppolite. The Haitian Family: Implications for the Sex
Education of Haitian Children in the United States. New York: Community
Society of New York, 1970.

0989. Souffrant, Claude. "Les Haitians aux Etats-Unis." Population, Special No.
29 (1974), p. 133ff.

0990. Stepick, Alex. "The New Haitian Exodus: The Flight from Terror and
Poverty." Caribbean Review, Vol. 11, No. 1 (Winter 1982), pp. 14-17, 55-57.

Traces Haitian history to examine the cause of emigration. These roots of
Haitian out-migration are discussed: the economy devastated by the
Revolution; the state dominated by an elite; a development strategy
benefiting the rich at the expense of the mass; corruption and repression
raised to new heights by the Duvalier regimes. The article concludes that
the Haitian migrants are truly both economic and political refugees.

0991. Verdet, P. "Trying Times: Haitian Youth in an Inner City High School."
Social Problems, Vol. 24, No. 2 (December 1976), pp. 228-233.

Describes the teaching of English and mathematics to Haitians at an inner
city high school in New England. Discusses the unique problems of
calculating in a foreign tongue, and the successes and failures at
communication by teachers and students.

0992.  Walsh, Bryan O.  "Haitians in Miami."  Migration Today, Vol. 7, No. 4 (1979).

0993.  Woldemikael, Teklemariam.  "Maintenance and Change of Status in a Migrant Community:  Haitians in Evanston, Illinois."  Ph. D. dissertation, Northwestern University, 1980.  333 pp. (DAI: 41/09A, p. 4178)

This study criticizes the concepts of assimilation and accomodation used in American social sciences.  Instead, it adopts Piaget's conceptual orientation to analyze the conflict of identity and status between the host and the migrant communities.  The findings indicate that the Haitians of Evanston insulate and create a marginal community with its own status and identity structure in the new surroundings while experiencing change in the second generation, which slowly becomes similar to the U.S.-born Afro-Americans.  The host society, on the other hand, makes a slight change to accomodate to the migrant community, while incorporating it into its social structure through the use of its existing social, economic, and political institutions.

0994.  Wortham, Jacob.  "The Black Boat People."  Black Enterprise, Vol. 10, No. 9 (April 1980), pp. 32, 34-35.

A brief note on Haitian refugees in Florida and their treatment by the Immigration service.

# VI.
# Select List of Works
# on Black Immigration To
# Canada and Great Britain

0995. Banton, MichaeL White and Coloured: The Behaviour of British People Toward Coloured Immigrants. London: Jonathan Cape, 1959.

0996. Benson, Susan. Ambiguous Ethnicity. Cambridge: Cambridge University Press, 1981.

0997. Blizzard, Flora H. West Indians in Canada. Guelph, Ont.: University of Guelph Library, 1970.

0998. Calley, M.J.C. God's People: West Indian Pentecostal Sects in England. London: Oxford University Press, 1965.

0999. Cheetham, Julia. Social Work with Immigrants. London: Routledge and Kegan Paul, 1972.

1000. Coard, Bernard. How the West Indian Child is Made Educationally Subnormal in the British School System. London: New Beacon Books, 1971.

1001. Davison, R.B. West Indian Migrants. London: Oxford University Press, 1962.

1002. Davison, R.B. Commonwealth Immigrants. London: Oxford University Press, 1964.

1003. Davison, R.B. Black British: Immigrants to England. London: Oxford University Press, 1966.

1004. Deakin, Nicholas. Colour, Citizenship and British Society. London: Panther Books, 1970.

1005. Field, Frank and Haikin, Patricia. Black Britons. London: Oxford University Press, 1971.

1006. Fitzherbert, Katrin. West Indian Children in London. London: G. Bell and Sons, 1967.

1007. Foner, Nancy. "The Meaning of Education to Jamaicans at Home and in London." New Community, VoL 4 (1975), pp. 195-202.

1008. Foner, Nancy. "Women, Work, and Migration: Jamaicans in London."
Urban Anthropology, Vol. 4 (1975), pp. 229-249.

1009. Foner, Nancy. "Male and Female: Jamaican Migrants in London."
Anthropological Quarterly, Vol. 49, No. 1 (1976), pp. 28-35.

1010. Foner, Nancy. "The Jamaicans: Cultural and Social Change Among Jamaicans
in Britain." In Between Two Cultures: Migrants and Minorities in Britain. Ed.,
James Watson. Oxford: Basil Blackwell, 1977.

1011. Foner, Nancy. Jamaica Farewell: Jamaican Migrants in London. Berkeley:
University of California Press, 1978.

1012. Freeman, Gary P. "Caribbean Migration to Britain and France: From
Assimilation to Selection." Caribbean Review, Vol. 11, No. 1 (Winter 1982), pp.
30-33, 61-64.

1013. Frideres, J.; Goldenberg, S. and Reeves, W. "The Economic Adaptation of
West Indians in Toronto." Canadian Review of Sociology and Anthropology, Vol.
15, No. 1 (February 1978), pp. 93-96.

1014. Gish, Oscar. "Color and Skill: British Immigration, 1955-1968." International Migration Review, Vol. 3 (1968), pp. 19-37.

1015. Glass, Ruth. Newcomers: The West Indian in London. London: Allen and
Unwin, 1960.

1016. Griffith, J.A.G. et al. Coloured Immigrants in Britain. London: Oxford
University Press, 1960.

1017. Handelman, Don. "Leadership, Solidarity, and Conflict in West Indian
Immigrant Associations (in Canada)." Human Organization, Vol. 26 (Fall 1967),
pp. 118-124.

1018. Henry, Frances. "The West Indian Domestic Scheme in Canada." Social
and Economic Studies, Vol. 17, No. 1 (March 1968), pp. 83-91.

1019. Henry, Frances. "A Note on Caribbean Migration to Canada." Caribbean
Review, Vol. 11, No. 1 (Winter 1982), pp. 38-41.

1020. Hill, Clifford. Immigration and integration: A Study of the Settlement of
Cloured Minorities in Britain. Oxford: Pergamon Press, 1970.

1021. Hill, Clifford. Black Churches: West Indian and African Sects in Britain.
London: Community and Race Relations Unit of the British Council of Churches,
1971.

1022. Hiro, Dilip. Black British, White British. New York: Monthly Review
Press, 1973.

1023. Holmes, Colin, ed. Immigrants and Minorities in British Society. London:
Allen and Unwin, 1978.

1024. Humphrey, Derek. Police Power and Black People. London: Panther Books,
1972.

1025. Humphrey, Derek and John, Gus. Because They Are Black. Baltimore: Penguin Books, 1971.

1026. Jadotte, Herard. "Haitian Immigration to Quebec." Journal of Black Studies, Vol. 7 (June 1977), pp. 485-500.

1027. Katznelson, Ira. Black Men, White Cities: Race, Politics, and Migration in the United States 1900-1930 and Britain 1948-1968. London: Oxford University Press, 1973.

1028. Lamur, Humphrey E. and Speckmann, John D., eds. Adaptation of Migrants from the Caribbean in the European and American Metropolis. Amsterdam: University of Amsterdam, 1976.

1029. Lawrence, Daniel. Black Migrants, White Natives: A Study of Race Relations in Nottingham. Cambridge: Cambridge University Press, 1974.

1030. Midgett, Douglas K. "West Indian Ethnicity in Great Britain." In Migration and Development. Eds., H.I. Safa and B.M. DuToit. The Hague: Mouton, 1975, pp. 57-81.

1031. Moore, Robert. Racism and Black Resistance in Britain. London: Pluto Press, 1975.

1032. Mullard, Chris. Black Britain. London: Allen and Unwin, 1973.

1033. Patterson, Sheila. Dark Strangers: A Study of West Indians in London. London: Tavistock, 1963.

1034. Patterson, Sheila. Immigration and Race Relations in Britain, 1960-1967. London: Oxford University Press, 1969.

1035. Peach, Ceri. West Indian Migration to Britain: A Social Geography. London: Oxford University Press, 1968.

1036. Peach, G.C.K. "West Indian Migration to Britain." International Migration Review, Vol. 1, No. 2 (Spring 1967), pp. 34-45.

1037. Pearson, David G. Race, Class and Political Activism: A Study of West Indians in Britain. London: Gower, 1981.

1038. Philpott, Stuart B. West Indian Migration: The Montserrat Case. London: Athlone Press, 1973.

1039. Pool, Gail R. "Development in the West Indies and Migration to Canada." Ph.D. dissertation, McGill University, 1979.

1040. Ramcharan, Subhas. "The Adaptation of West Indian Immigrants in Canada." Ph.D. dissertation, York University, 1974.

1041. Ramcharan, Subhas. "The Economic Adaptation of West Indians in Toronto, Canada." Canadian Review of Sociology and Anthropology, Vol. 13, No. 3 (August 1976), pp. 295-304.

1042. Rex, John. Colonial Immigrants in a British City. London: Routledge and Kegan Paul, 1979.

1043.  Richmond, Anthony H.  _Post-War Immigrants in Canada._  Toronto:  University of Toronto Press, 1967.

1044.  Richmond, Anthony H.  _Migration and Race Relations in an English City._  London: Oxford University Press, 1973.

1045.  Rose, E.J.B. et al.  _Colour and Citizenship: A Report on British Race Relations._  London: Oxford University Press, 1969.

1046.  Ruck, S.K., ed.  _The West Indian Comes to England._  London: Routledge and Kegan Paul, 1960.

1047.  Sivanandan, A.  "Race, Class and the State:  The Black Experience in Britain."  _Race and Class,_ Vol. 17 (1976), pp. 356-368.

1048.  Turrittin, Jane Sawyer.  "Networks and Mobility:  The Case of West Indian Domestics from Montserrat."  _Canadian Review of Sociology and Anthropology,_ Vol. 13, No. 3 (August 1976), pp. 305-320.

1049.  Wright, Peter L.  _The Coloured Worker in British Industry._  London:  Oxford University Press, 1968.

# Subject Index

# Author Index

## About the Center for Afroamerican and African Studies

The Center for Afroamerican Studies at the University of Michigan is the focal point for the comparative and interdisciplinary analysis of the black experience in Africa and the Americas. The Center provides a forum for discussion, a catalyst for research collaboration, and a rich, comprehensive curriculum designed to meet a broad spectrum of student needs and interests.